COACHES CLINICS

MAN-TO-MAN
DEFENSE

Edited by
Bob Murrey

ISBN: 1-57167-429-2
Library of Congress Catalog Card Number: 1-57167-429-2

Cover Design: Jennifer Scott
Cover Photo: Courtesy of the University of Utah
Series Editor: Deborah M. Bellaire
Production Manager: Michelle A. Summers

Coaches Choice Books is a division of:
    Sagamore Publishing, Inc.
    P.O. Box 647
    Champaign, IL 61824-0647
    http://www.sagamorepub.com

TABLE OF CONTENTS

DIAGRAM LEGEND

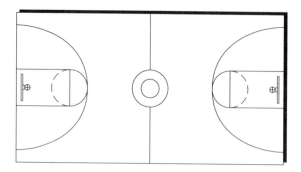

PLAYERS

(5) Centers

(3, 4) Forwards

(1, 2) Guards

◯ = **Offense**

X = **Defense**

◔ = **Player with the Ball**

– – → = **Direct Pass**

⊢ = **Screen**

〜〜→ = **Dribble**

──→ = **Cut of Player Without Ball**

╫╫╫╫→ = **Shot**

Chapter One

BUILDING A DEFENSE

J.D. Barnett

I have a tremendous amount of difficulty in getting players to pass the ball correctly. When they shoot, they look to see if it goes in. When they pass, they are going someplace trying to figure out how to get the ball back. So they never look to see where the ball goes. I say this a thousand times at practice. "A good pass leads to a made shot. A poor pass leads to no shot." How many times do you see a man come off a screen and get a pass that he can't handle cleanly? With the use of the Toss Back, we become aware of a bad pass. If you give the Toss Back a poor pass, you get a poor pass in return. Players don't like to chase balls. The other thing that it does is it makes the player go to the ball. They can pass it, and then they must move to catch it. We use it during the summer for our "self-improvement program." A player only needs a ball, a Toss Back, and a basket. I don't work for Toss Back, but I do believe that it is a good apparatus. I also use the "Big Ball." It weighs the same as the regular ball, but it is bigger. We used it with players who were poor free throw shooters. It was great for hand placement.

I would like to ask you what you try to do at the defensive end of the floor? Does your team understand what you are trying to accomplish? I only have so many markers to use up. I can only get on them so many times, so I try to be very selective about those times. The older we get, the more we learn how to **respond** rather than to **react**. Don't react, learn to respond. Be able to communicate. Fighting is a reaction, walking away is a response.

At the end of our first practice there will be **three things** very clear to our players, and they will be able to tell you what we are trying to get done. We do not give up layups, we do not give up second shots, and we learn to contest shots. They may not learn anything else that day, but they will have heard these three things so many times during the course of one practice that they will hear them as they go into the locker room.

Here are our rules:

- Contest every shot.

- Retreat quickly to the ball line. (Diagram 1) The ball line is a line parallel to the endline at the point of the ball.

- We allow no penetrating passes lower than this line.

- We also allow all non-penetrating passes.

- Always see the ball and your man.

- Try to intercept any lob or bounce passes.

- Jump to the ball on every pass.

- Maintain proper sag position in relation to the ball.

- Trap the ball in the low post.

- Keep pressure on the ball at all times.

- Never foul a man who is not an offensive threat.

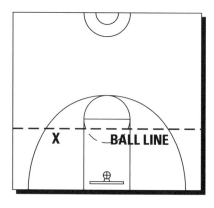

Diagram 1

I'm going to give you our **teaching techniques** and why we do what we do. We play one arm length away. From that distance we can put pressure on the ball and at the same time keep from allowing penetration. We are on the inside shoulder, the inside hand up, and the other hand back. Inside foot is up. We used to try to mirror the ball with both hands, but found that we were getting high. We lost our balance, the most important thing in defense. You then lose the ability to react. This causes more fouls. We want the knees bent, heel to toe, and one hand traces the ball with the up hand. Our feet are stable. We do not want the weight on the balls of the feet. We want the weight evenly distributed so that you can go forward or backward with the same degree of quickness. If you think about the game most of the time, you play it moving backwards. But on closeouts you are moving forward. Closeouts are becoming more of a factor as the 3-point shot develops.

There is a definite **correlation** between **ball pressure and post feed**. On defense we try to keep the back straight and the nose on the ball. We want them to constantly turn the ball. We want them to turn the ball five times in 94 feet. If we do that, we will get a minimum of two possibilities of doubling. We are looking for the double team. The rule is that the ball can't see you. Anytime the ball can't see you, we never trap up, we trap across. If a player leans forward, he is more easily penetrated. If you have great athletes, they can make mistakes because they can recover. If you have marginal athletes, they can't make mistakes. We have the palm up on the front hand in the full-court game. We say, **"Dig, don't go for the ball, just dig."** We keep the hand outside the knee, trying to get a deflection. Off the ball, one pass away we play as close to the ball as we can play. We don't play close to the man when we are trying stop a guard-to-forward pass because we feel that we are vulnerable to a hard fake to the midsection, and he can step back and receive the ball. So we get off the ball as much as we can without allowing the ball to go over our head. Our rule is to take your knee and put it in the midsection of the receiver. He should **see both ball and man.** Put the thumb down, palm up, and bend the elbow. This may cause an interception. You can't intercept with the back hand because if you don't get it, you are really beat. So use the lead hand. On any back cut, you play until you lose sight of your man, then open up to the ball. You must recover quickly because of the 3-point shot. After the ball is caught, the inside foot and hand are forward. Put as much pressure as possible on the ball and whoever was guarding the passer jumps to the ball and **backpedals** to the ball line. All of our doubles will come from on top.

The pros do three things. They either double on top, double from the wing, or have a designated trapper. Out of that, they will double on the first pass or on the dribble. We double from on top. If the ball is above the free-throw line or above me, I am highside with a lot of contact. We use an arm bar with a closed fist. (Note: Arm bar is when the arm from elbow to shoulder is horizontal.) Officials don't call what they see, they call what they think they see. If you open your hand, they have the tendency to call a hold. So, keep your fist closed.

As the ball would go below, we start moving on the daylight of the pass or the dribble. We step over the top and turn our back on the ball to get to the lowside. This is the only time we tell players they can turn their back to the ball. We have different post people play the post in different ways. We have some quick, smaller kids. So he fronts. We have a 7' kid. He plays behind because he isn't strong. When he tried to play on the side, he got moved up and pinned. When we front, we put the left leg in the crouch of the post. Put the other leg on the highside and sit on the top leg of the post. **Keep your hands above your eyes.** On any shot, he should go to the dotted area and get inside the post. So, play topside if the ball is above you, bottomside if the ball is below, front if you have the quickness, or behind if you lack strength. In general we get behind if the post is at the second hash mark or higher. Our rule on sag is small of the back to the baseline. When the ball is above the foul line, one step to the manside.

(Diagram 2) When the ball is below the foul line, get on the **midline.** The **midline** extends from top of key to front of rim. The two sides are ballside and helpside. If you are on the ballside, you overplay and help. If you are away, you help. We are guarding the ball. We are not guarding a man. You have a man responsibility, but the first and foremost thing is the ball.

(Diagram 3) This is the scoring area. Anytime the ball gets into this area, we want two on the ball. We will trap by using the closest man on top.

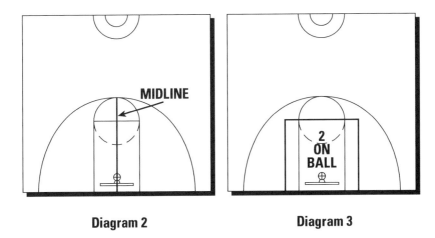

Diagram 2   **Diagram 3**

(Diagram 4) We are playing **behind** the post. If the ball is on the wing, this should be our defensive position, I don't care where the offensive players are. The ball is below the foul line. The man guarding the post is to take away the baseline. Don't go for the pass. We trap with the closest man on top. The other top man drops to the ball line and splits the difference between the ball and the next available receiver with his back to the baseline. Don't triple, we only want a double. This man is called the x man, and is responsible for the first pass out.

(Diagram 5) We call this the 1, 2, and 3 zones.

(Diagram 6) The ball is into the **post.** We have two on the ball. We want to move on daylight between the ball and the passer. That's when we move. If I'm on top and I see the ball leave, my responsibility is double team. By the time the ball is caught, I want to put my chest on the elbow of the post. I want to be on top of him with my chest. If his elbow is down, I try to pin it down. It it's up, I am underneath him, but I am on him so he cannot drop his lead leg. We don't want him to be able to see the entire floor. Get the hands pointed to the sky and push. If the post had been fronting, on the pass, if you are not positive that you can intercept, you roll and get baseline side. When X3 sees the ball go into the post from his man, he jumps to the ball and becomes a **digger.** He must also be responsible for the pass back out to the corner. We find that the shooting against us is much more effective from both corners than it is from the top.

Diagram 4

Diagram 5

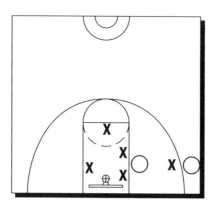

Diagram 6

(Diagram 7) If the ball is shot from the corner, chances are that the rebound is either coming straight back or going straight over. If it goes straight over, we only have one man there, and they may have two men on the backside. So they have a 2/1 advantage most of the time. We try to keep the shot from being taken from the corner on the ballside.

(Diagram 8) Our split man (X2) has the 1 zone. Pass out, and for rule of organization, we tell the trapper to **follow** the pass out. But the majority of the time X2 will go to the pass. This allows us to locate the ball and the man.

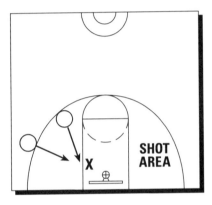

Diagram 7

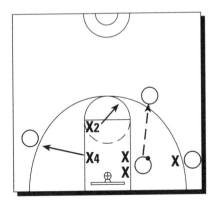

Diagram 8

(Diagram 9) If X2 takes the ball, we make the X move with the man who doubled down taking the center area. **Never, never leave home (X4).** We never want X4 coming high. We have no rebounder, no blockout man, so never leave home. It becomes an X trapping situation.

(Diagram 10) One reason that we double with the closest player on top is because of the **angle.** The move of the post is normal to the middle of the floor because he sees the baseline already taken away, so we try to **trap** quickly. We want the double to occur as the ball is caught. Everyone talks about offensive spacing. How much do you talk about defensive spacing? They can get there even if they are slow if they begin from the ball line. We are allowing all **reversal passing.**

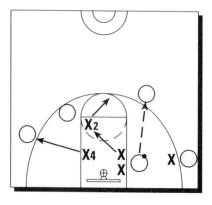
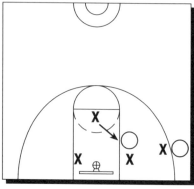

Diagram 9   **Diagram 10**

(Diagram 11) We cannot stop this pass and double at the same time. **You cannot ask them to do more than they are able.** They will become frustrated. Remember, when you double down, don't try to steal the ball, get your hands straight in the air. **"Palms to the sky."** Don't try to steal the ball. We want to get it done as a team. Don't do your individual thing. We shot 44.7% and won 118 games, so we must have been doing something right somewhere.

If you will give this some thought, figure what works for you, commit yourself to double teams in the post, to closeouts and contesting, I contend you will be a good defensive team. There are some players who, when the ball goes in, it never comes out and when you double them, they have some problems. You will get some charges from this. Don't go for the steal, we want the ball passed back out.

(Diagram 12) X2 is the only man with his back to the ball. **He is actually running a zone.** If there is a cutter, he must check him. X2 is looking, but not turning. When the ball comes out, X2 goes to the ball. X1 must "X." X1 takes one step toward the ball, and then picks up other man because we must have the blockouts. We don't want to give up second shots.

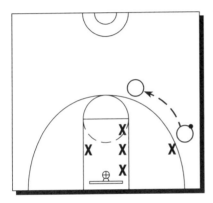

Diagram 11

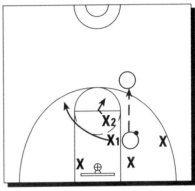

Diagram 12

(Diagram 13) On the dribble, we double down and everyone else rotates to the ball line with the same rules. The **trapper** follows the pass out. We rotate for backside rebounding. We play the ball on the inside shoulder, forcing to the sideline. Everything we do footwise, we do with back foot first. If I am playing the man with the ball and he drives, my first move is back foot open. This means that I step back with my back foot first, and then with the front foot. We try to emphasize movement, get some distance, open up and stop the ball. **The whole game is angles.** You aren't guarding the man, you are guarding the ball and you are trying keep the ball from going where they can score with it. Most players cannot score off of the first dribble.

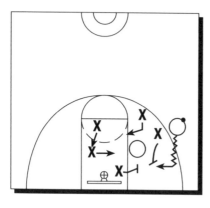

Diagram 13

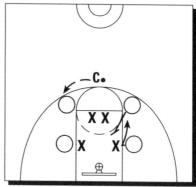

Diagram 14

(Diagram 14) **Screens**. C is the coach. 4/4. Pass, screen down. We do thin side, ballside of all screens.

(Diagram 15) The man guarding the screen jumps back, comes down, and lets the player who is being screened go through. The player who is guarding the screener must now get his lead leg over the lead leg of the screener. The player being screened must stay in the passing lane.

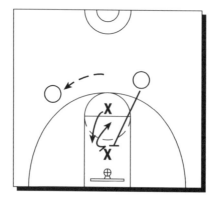

Diagram 15

(Diagram 16) **Flex cut** on the baseline. Screendown takes place. Go high or low off of the screen. I call this **SWAG.** I sag to the middle of the back of the screener. The person being screened must jump to the ballside, but he needs help. If it is a penetrating pass, we overplay the pass. If it is not a penetrating pass, we allow the pass to be made.

(Diagram 17) **Cross-screens.** Consider this. Cross-screens on the ball instead of away from the ball.

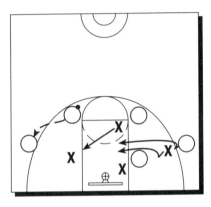

Diagram 16

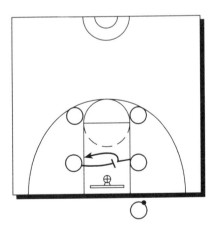

Diagram 17

(Diagram 18) We run an **offensive set.** We may not get the person open who was screened, but we get the ball on the block.

(Diagram 19) On a **cross-screen**, we do not switch, we sag. We go ballside and re-establish. I don't like our players taking shortcuts, and when they switch, they are taking shortcuts. And on the down screens, you can end up little on big and you have a mismatch. You can also double the ball when there is a switch on the ball. This is especially effective when the point guard is small.

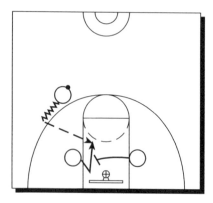

Diagram 18

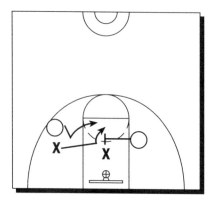

Diagram 19

Chapter Two

UMASS DEFENSIVE PHILOSOPHY

John Calipari

I hope when people watch us play, they say, "Boy, do they play hard." "Boy, do they play scrappy." The things we emphasize in practice in regard to our defense are:

- **Competitive drills**—we want head-to-head competition.

- **Peer Pressure drills**—if one player messes up, all players suffer for it. This happens in a game, so why not in practice? If you don't watch this, it can become negative. Instead of building each other up, they could wind up tearing each other down.

- **Key Words**—Tony Mason gave me this idea. I don't want to stop play to talk. I want players to have to **play through things.** Assign different coaches different terms they are to emphasize that day. Terms such as, "Ball pressure, ball pressure;" "No splits, no splits;" "Cheat up, cheat up." Players have been educated in what these terms mean, so when they hear these key words, they know what to do.

Some offensive and defensive pet peeves I have are:

- Catching the ball or rebounding the ball with **one hand.** We stop practice and have all run; **peer pressure.**

- **Look-away passes.**

- **Run-throughs**—player goes to steal a pass, misses it, and is completely out of the play. Our goal is to be **last** in steals in the league but **first** in defensive field goal percentage and rebounding.

Our defensive goals are:

- **Great ball pressure**—we want the offensive player to have to dribble, we tell our players, "Make the guy prove he can play."

- **No splits**—if I'm going to make my man dribble, I have to have teammates ready to help. If my offensive man is outside the three-point line, I'll let him catch the ball. It is the help man's responsibility to stop the drive.

- **Get around the post**—the defensive man's foot and arm are on the line of the ball to the post. We do not front!

- **Weakside position**

Whenever we do a defensive drill, we emphasize these four things.

We don't do a lot on **denial** because we are concerned about the split. We break our defensive drills into five areas. They are:

- One-on-one defense

- Two-on-two defense

- Series defense (three-on-three)

- Shell drill

- Five-on-five team defense

ONE-ON-ONE DRILLS:

- **Mirror drill.**

  This is a one-on-one **stationary** drill. We have an offensive and a defensive player. We are working on **ball pressure.** We have the offensive man start with the ball above his head. The defensive man should then attack the ball all out. When the ball is brought down, we tell our players to follow the ball with the hand, but as the ball goes lower than the waist, we want our defenders to take one step back to stop a potential drive. We divide the team in half and we go two to three minutes.

- **Contain and Contest.**

  (Diagram 1) The defense passes to the offense and moves to guard him. The defender must **contain** his man, **contest** the shot, and **rebound**. We don't allow the offense to use the dribble in this drill. We do this from three different spots on the floor.

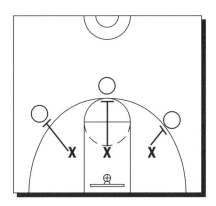

Diagram 1

- **Contain and Contest with Dribble.**

  (Diagram 2) Here the offense dribbles at the defender and the defender must contain the dribble, contest any shot, and rebound.

- **Pass, Cut, Reverse, One-on-One.**

  (Diagram 3) In this drill, we place three players on offense. We have the point pass to the wing and make a cut to the basket. The defender must jump to the ball and **deny** a return pass. The offensive player then cuts through to the weakside. The ball is reversed to the offside wing. The defender must follow his man through, stopping in the lane in **helpside** position. On the ball reversal, he must get to his man and **contain and contest.**

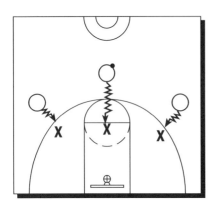
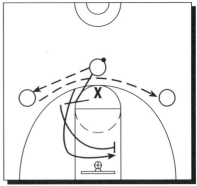

Diagram 2   **Diagram 3**

- **Zigzag Drill with Tap Drill.**

  (Diagram 4) We start with a normal zigzag. The coach standing at the corner of half-court then calls for the ball and starts to dribble to the basket. The defensive player in the zigzag drill must come up from behind the coach and tap the ball away. When he achieves this, the manager standing by the center circle passes a ball to the offense who stopped after making the pass to the coach. Upon catching the ball, he dribbles hard for the basket and the defender must hustle to pick him up and **close out** on defense.

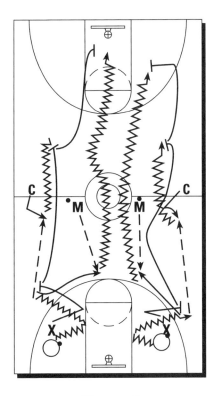

Diagram 4

TWO-ON-TWO DRILLS:

- **Screen Down Drill.**

  (Diagram 5)   When a team screens down, we have our man being screened **chase** his man over the screen. We do this because we are not worried about stealing the ball, just getting **pressure** on the ball. If they curl against this, it is the defender on the screener's responsibility to stop the curl.

(Diagram 6) On backscreens and doublescreens we don't switch, we **chase through.**

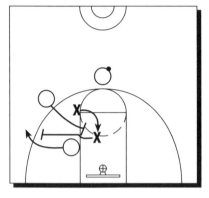 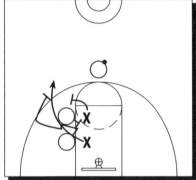

Diagram 5   **Diagram 6**

- **Cross Screen Drill.**

(Diagram 7) We line up two offensive men on the blocks, each being guarded. The ball starts on top and is taken to one wing or the other. The man to whose side the ball comes, becomes the **screener** and the man away becomes the **cutter.** On cross-screens we do switch, but we tell our players if we are going to switch, we don't allow the cutter to catch the ball. If we are going to allow the man to catch the ball, why did we switch?

SERIES DRILLS:

- **3-on-3 Flex.**

(Diagram 8) We set up in the flex offense with 1 at the guard, 2 on the block, and 3 in the corner. 1 passes the ball to the coach/manager in the offside guard position and we run the **flex cut.** We tell our defensive man on 3 to make sure he comes over top of the screen and not allow him to go high and come low off the screen.

We fight over the screen and don't allow our defender to go behind. We rotate our players so they play each position on offense and defense.

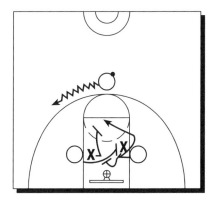

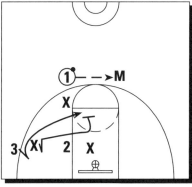

Diagram 7   **Diagram 8**

• **3-on-3 UCLA.**

(Diagram 9) Here we work on the famed UCLA cut that we see quite a bit. We rotate our offense into the spots shown so if the first cut doesn't result in a shot, we keep running this move until the defense gets the ball on a turnover or rebound.

Diagram 9

- **Double Down.**

  (Diagrams 10-14) You can run this from many different sets, as shown in these diagrams. The ball starts at the top of the key and is dribbled off to the side. Our rules on the double-down are that the defender on 5 is to stop the curl move, the defender on 4 is to stop 5 from cutting to the basket for a post up, 2's defender is to get over top of the screen and stay with his man.

Diagram 10

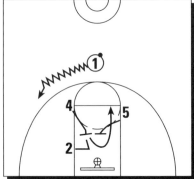

Diagram 11

Diagram 12

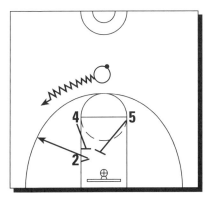

Diagram 13

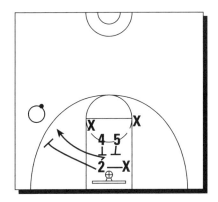

Diagram 14

Chapter Three

INDIANA DEFENSE

Dan Dakich

Defense is important to most teams if they want to be competitive. But, at Indiana, **good** defense is absolutely essential—and expected. If you don't play good defense, you don't play—period. Be demanding, not demeaning.

Reasons for Playing Strictly Man-to-Man

- It promotes aggressiveness.

- It is the best of both worlds—man defense along with help and zone principles.

- Zero in on only one thing.

You can't beat the best teams with a press, only mediocre teams.

Points to Be Achieved on Defense

- Get back, stop the ball, protect the basket.

  - The first player back must be as deep as the offensive man.

  - Protect the basket before stopping the ball.

- Establish who your man is.

- Pressure the ball to distort the offense.

  —Know your personnel.

    - Where to pick up the ball.

    - Who should contest the shot.

    - Where the shot should be contested.

- Take away **ball reversal.**

- Fake trap—slows penetrations.

- Control radius.

  —Fighting with posts.

  —Helping and taking away cuts.

- Arrive at the same point the offense does when he catches the ball.

- Block out—Rebound.

Keep the ball out of the middle area of the floor. You must talk and communicate constantly with your teammates.

Always be on balance.

You cannot afford to lunge at the ball.

On help—the defense is one step on the **manside** (above the free-throw line extended)—the defense is one step on the **ballside** (below the free-throw line extended)

You must constantly guard against being lazy.

Keep your head on a swivel.

When a pass is made, everyone jumps to the ball.

When a player is guarding the man with the ball, and he then makes a pass, everyone jumps to the ball.

Everything is dictated by the basketball. The ball is like a book; the player must read it. On defense, **play the ball.** On offense, **play your man.**

Individual Defense

- Proper stance—with constant movement for quick recovery.

- Balance—use quick, choppy steps.

  —Full-court zigzag drills.

  —Pair up equally.

Ball Pressure/Contesting

- Make team backcut.

- Guard to wing—classic see ball and man.

- Guard to guard—open up preventing penetration.

Help and Recover

- Stop the ball.

- Position—short, low, then hand up for the shot.

Only play head up when recovering. The rest of the time **force** the ball to the **side** of the court.

When you are playing a zone, distort it when you have the numbers. Our defense does the same thing.

Post Defense

- Force the post out two steps farther than the offense wants to play.

- Once the post catches the ball, back off until he makes a move, then contest.

- If the ball is below the free-throw line, play on the low side.

- If the ball is above the free-throw line, the defense plays on the high side.

Switching screens slows down the offense.

Defending Ball Screens

- Underneath

- Step out—basically setting a double screen

Each individual defensive drill is two minutes.

Each team defensive drill is five minutes.

Lunging at the offense not only is a poor play, it is a dumb play.

Drills

- Zigzag

- Driving line—keep the offense from getting to the middle of the court

- Contesting—also working on rotation, 1-on-1, 2-on-2

- 1-on-1 Post play—coach making the pass

- 2-on-2 using cross-screens, high and low

- 3-on-3 giving players more room to move—rebound

- 5-on-4 defense and 6-on-4 defense—working on communication skills with the offense and defense

- 5-man change drill—call "change"—the offense drops the ball and becomes the defense (cannot guard the man you were guarding)

Defense Checklist

- Giving up easy points

- Fouling too much

- Are we difficult to play against?

- Are we pressuring the ball?

- Are we distorting their offense?

- How tough is it to get inside?

- Are we forcing the ball to the corner?

- Percent of the opponent's shots are under pressure.

- How many second shots are given up?

(Diagram 1) **Fake trap.** B comes up as if he is going to trap 1 with the help of C. B quickly moves back to cover.

(Diagram 2) **Contesting.** The defense allows only two dribbles as they force the ball to the sideline or into a trap.

(Diagram 3) This is an excellent drill to teach your defense they must work hard and be aggressive. The two corner men must stay there. They can shoot or pass.

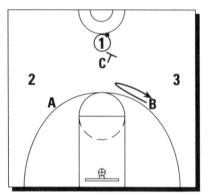

Diagram 1

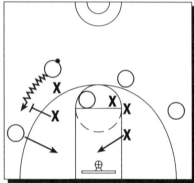

Diagram 2

Diagram 3

(Diagram 4) We divide the front court into four areas. Players know where the helpside area is located. They cover the next potential receiver tight.

(Diagram 5) Two coaches or managers each have a ball. When 1 receives the ball, he can shoot or pass back to C or M. 1 moves to get open for the best pass.

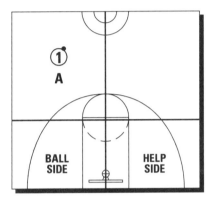

Diagram 4

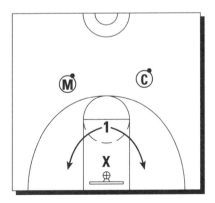

Diagram 5

Chapter Four

MAN-TO-MAN DEFENSE

Mike Jarvis

The Definition of Defense

Webster defines aggressiveness as **"the disposition to dominate."**
For us to win, we feel our defense must dominate the offense. We want
the offense doing what we want; not what they want. Therefore, just
as some defenses are built on quickness, size or strength, ours is
built on aggressiveness, teamwork and intelligence. We feel that
while not everyone can be quick, big, or strong, there is no reason
why each of our players can't be extremely aggressive, intelligent
and play as a team. Be prepared for drills that create and teach the
above. It must be instinctive for us to dive on the floor for loose
balls; feel and believe that every loose ball is ours, take the charge,
and be more physical, aggressive and intelligent than our opponent.

Defensive Beliefs

We will play **aggressive**, intelligent defense with a **"we"** mentality.
We want our five men to work at and believe in the principle that it truly
is a **team effort.** It's our five men against the ball.

We will combine what we feel are the best parts of zone and
man-to-man defense, placing our primary focus on the ball rather than a
man or an area. It is the responsibility of each and every defensive player
to **stop the ball**.

Our defensive vocabulary begins with the words **"ballside"** and
"weakside." Ballside simply refers to that half of the court where
the ball is. **Weakside** refers to the other half of the court. Players on
the weakside must be ready to help stop the ball at all times. Our

ballside defense is responsible for putting immediate and constant pressure on the man with the ball. It must also prevent or contest the **penetrating** passes toward the basket we are defending. At the same time, those players on the **weakside** must be in position to aid in **preventing penetration** of the ball. Their primary responsibility and the focal point of their attention is the ball and not the man.

In order to compete for the Atlantic 10 Championships, we must play excellent man-to-man defense.

Ballside Defense

A. Stance and movement on the ball.

1. Stance.

   a. We want to keep our feet at least shoulder-width apart.

   b. The foot we place forward will depend on the offensive player. If the offensive man is right-handed, we put the left leg forward with the heel of the left foot in front of the toes of the right foot and vice versa.

   c. The extended leg is outside his strong leg, forcing the offensive player to dribble with his weak hand.

   d. The body is bent at the knees and **not at the waist.** The back is at a 60-degree angle to the floor as are the upper parts of the legs (quads).

   e. The forearms are parallel: the elbows are bent slightly and the hands are positioned **just inside the knees.**

   f. Our feet provide us with our base and we want to put our weight forward, on the balls of our feet.

g. On defense we must **control** the first step of the offensive man. When the offensive man drops the ball below the shoulder, we retreat an additional arm's-length off the ball. Think of taking two half-steps, as we do when we shuffle properly.

The same movement in the **reverse** direction occurs when the offensive man returns to the shooting position. So we must be prepared to retreat, then attack. If the ball is up in shooting position, **"attack."** If the ball is lowered into penetrating position, **"retreat."**

When we **"attack,"** the lead hand should be up to bother the shot.

When we **"retreat,"** the lead hand should be lowered to bother the dribbler.

h. When we shuffle vs. the dribble, we take a series of **half-steps**. Our first half-step is with the foot nearest the direction in which we are going. For example, if we shuffle left, our first half-step is with our left foot, then we take a half-step with our right foot. This will enable us to maintain the proper distance between our feet and a good wide base as we described in (a).

i. Once the ball touches the floor, we apply constant pressure on the ball. **In the backcourt,** we want to turn the dribbler as many times as we can before he crosses the mid-court line. The first thing we want to do is force the dribbler to put the ball on the floor with his weak hand. For example, if he were right-handed, we would position ourselves arm's-length distance from the dribbler with our left leg outside of his right foot. Our right leg would be in the drop-step position. We continue to bother the dribbler with the lead hand, trying to get the lead hand under the ball, palms up. Try to get the lead foot, hand, and head in line with the ball. If the dribbler changes direction, we execute a drop-step. When the dribbler uses his right hand, we have our right hand and right foot forward. If the dribbler uses his left hand, we are bothering the ball with our left hand and our left hand is forward.

The Discontinued Dribble

"Countdown"

After we have attacked and pressured the ball and have made the offensive man discontinue his dribble, our job is only half done. **DON'T RELAX - Attack the ball "Belly Up."**

Try not to let the man pass the ball. Move those hands and arms (windmill), yell, don't reach, get that five-second count.

Count out Loud "5" - "5" - "5" - "5" - "5"

Points of Emphasis

1. The defensive man plays as **tight** as he can without getting beat. Don't be afraid to get burned once or twice before you know how close you can play.

2   We assume a **boxer's stance** (heel of lead foot is aligned with toe of back foot).

3. The hands, **palms up**, apply constant pressure to the ball when the ball is dribbled beyond shooting range. **Palms down** when playing the ball in scoring position.

4. Force the dribbler to go to his **weak** hand first.

5.   If the offensive man **turns his back** on a reverse dribble, the defensive man must retreat one step to avoid getting caught by the offensive **drop-step** and assume head-to-head alignment.

6. Don't **cross** your feet when moving or changing direction.

7. The feet never stop moving - stutter step - as you play defense. Step-step, step-step, take a **half-step** with the outside foot (left going left), then step with the other foot. Keep your feet **spread** apart at all times.

8. **Attack** the ball - don't wait for it to be dribbled.

9. After attacking the ball, we want the offensive man to discontinue his dribble. When this occurs, ALL FIVE MEN **deny** their man the ball and attempt to get the five-second call.

Countdown: "5" - "5" - "5" - "5"

10. The **toes** of the lead foot point in the direction you are going.

11. Remember to be **off the man** (arm's length) and in a head -to -head alignment if he hasn't dribbled or turns his back to you.

12. Stay up on the **balls** of your feet.

13. If beaten, turn and **run** until you get ahead of the ball.

In the Backcourt

1. Make the dribbler use his **weak** hand first.

2   Then pressure the ball and turn him, trying to make him **change direction** as much as possible.

3. Left hand and left foot are advanced vs. left-hand dribble and vice versa.

4   If beaten, turn and run.

5   Continue to **apply pressure** and remember to turn the man until he crosses half-court. Then continually force him to use his weak hand. When he attempts to go to his strong hand, take it away and force him back to his weak hand.

Bothering the Shooter

1. Whether you leave your feet or not, we want your **hand on the ball** and not in the shooter's face. We feel that forcing the shooter to

adjust his shot is more detrimental to good shooting than obstructing his vision. However, this may vary from player to player, so pay close attention to scouting reports.

2. The hand **nearest** the shooter's hand (left vs. right) must be raised above the shoulder, and from here it only has to be raised a short distance. This also decreases the chance of fouling.

3. The legs are slightly bent at the knees, ready to react to the leap of the shooter. From this position, we can use defensive fakes and possibly force the offensive man to **hurry** his shot.

4. If you do leave your feet to bother the shooter, the hand and arm are extended straight up, not into the shooter. The hand is in line with the ball. The ball comes to the hand.

5. Stay **on your feet** until your opponent leaves his.

6   Don't go for the **fake**.

7. When you attack the man with the ball, get off him about arm's length and **move** those feet (stutter).

Blocking Out

We believe that the **two most overrated things in basketball are size and jumping ability**. Position is by far the most important part in rebounding.

1. Making Contact

    We feel that it is essential to make **contact** with the offensive man to keep him off the boards. We stress the following points.

In Low and Mid-Post

    a. Pivot and keep the **elbows** as high as the shoulders with the hands raised. This greatly widens the block-out area and puts the hands in a position where they can't **hold**.

b.   Make **contact** with the butt, hitting the offensive man in the upper legs.

c.   Take a **half-step** back into the man. **Never** take your eye off the ball when blocking out. See the ball—touch your man—go get the ball.

2.   Get the Ball

a .   After executing the above, you now can get the ball.

b.   Go strong to the ball and prepare to make the transition from defense to offense.

3.   Yell **"Ball"** on the rebound to initiate the break.

4.   The further your man is **away** from the basket, the less of a **threat** he is to rebound.

5   Contact must be made, sustained and maintained as long as necessary when defending a man in the three-second lane. Try to **force** your man out of the lane with your butt.

Fighting over the Top

We have to work on this, especially if we do not want to **switch** guard to forward.

The defensive man must get **good pressure** on the ball to **force** the dribbler away from the screen. Don't let him get to the screen. Keep bothering the ball from the floor up, coming up under the ball with the palm of the hand.

Make him change direction—get in his path.

At first we expect the defensive man to fight **over the top** of the screen on his own, and later we will provide defensive help from the forward.

Technique

When contact is made with the pick, step over the pick and straighten up, making yourself as small as possible, then **slide** through. Upon sliding through, assume the proper defensive stance. Contact should be made with the hand nearest the pick. Later on, you will get verbal help.

Try to prevent the man from using the pick by **forcing** him to go in the opposite direction.

Feel with the hand **nearest** the pick.

If unable to change the dribbler's direction, the hand makes initial contact, **step over the pick**, straighten up and slide through. Once you get through, reassume defensive stance.

Chapter Five

MAN-TO-MAN DEFENSE

Jim Johnson

Five Basic Reasons:

- Most teams have one or two big scorers. We don't see many teams that have four or five big scorers. I want my best defensive players on their scorers. I want the match-up I want. If I am playing zone, I can't do that. You can always **hide** one player on defense. That's one of the first things I do when I scout. "Where am I going to hide her?"

- We don't want players to stand and shoot. I don't want our players to just stand there. I want them to have to come off the pick or shoot off the dribble. I don't want them comfortable.

- **Blocking out.** I hate giving up easy points, and offensive rebounds are easy baskets. We played some 1-3-1 this year, and I always cringed. I didn't like it because I didn't know whose fault it was when someone wasn't blocked out. With man-to-man, I know.

- Even if you do play zone, at some point, you have to cover man-to-man. If you know how to play man-to-man, you can play zone. My JV team only plays man-to-man.

- A man-to-man is **flexible.** You can extend it, you can sag it, you can create pressure. We have sagged so much that people thought we were playing zone.

Nine Principles

There are nine things that we must do if we are going to play man-to-man.

- **We must be in good condition.** Games are 32 minutes; you will be on defense for half of it, so for 16 minutes you must be able to be in your defensive stance. We don't normally do a lot of "just running," but we work hard in our **defensive drills**.

- **Attitude.** I think that we must be cocky. We must think that we are in control. We are not going to react; we are going to dictate what you can or cannot do. The players must have that attitude.

- **Habits.** People talk about muscle memory in shooting so why not for defensive drills? We do things over and over and form habits. I have all my drills on cards. My defensive stack is by far the thickest. Habits must be formed.

- **They must believe.** You must get into their heads, convince them they are a good defensive team. We want to convince them that we are going to win because we play better defense than anybody else. They must play with heart and desire. If they don't have that, then we haven't done a very good job. You must get into their heads when they are freshmen.

- **See your player all the time**. This is different from many others. Many people say don't lose the ball. We never lose our player. If the person I am guarding cuts, I follow her; I don't open up to the ball.

- Every time the **ball** moves, the **defense** must move. If you haven't moved, something is wrong. If you haven't moved, you are not in good position.

- **Communication**, not only with each other but with the staff. Do they understand the terms you use?

- **Never give up the baseline**, never, never, ever!

- **Scouting Reports.** I have an assistant coach who is a scouting fiend. So much of what we do is based on his reports. If you have good scouting reports, you can adjust your man-to-man defense. We started giving out two-page scouting reports and our kids want them. I have seen them quiz each other in the locker room before a game.

What We Want for Each Position

Point Guard

We want **pressure** on the ball, arm distance away, especially in practice. They will get beat in practice, but keep them up there. They must be on their toes. Usually we pick up around the three-point line. This will vary depending on whom we are guarding. Don't let that ballhandler penetrate. I don't care if my point guard never steals the ball, but I don't want the ball to penetrate.

After the ball is passed, they must **jump** ballside. I don't want the offensive player to cut between my player and the ball. I want to make her cut behind. I don't care where she goes on a cut to the weakside.

Strongside Wing

Deny the ball out to the three-point line. This varies with the opponent. Put your ear in the opponent's chest.

If the wing does get the ball, **slide down** and **protect the baseline.** Have the defensive player at least one- half person on the baseline side. The foot of our defensive player is between the legs of the offensive player. If she breaks into the middle, we will drop-step and go straight across the lane. We hope to have help from the point guard position.

If there is penetration from the point, we want to **help and recover** from the wing position. Put one hand in the face of the dribbler, the other hand in the passing lane. I don't want the defensive player to come up to help. I want the wing to be able to help and recover.

If the ball goes into the post, we double-down unless the wing is a shooter.

Strongside Post

When the ball is at the point, defend the middle. **"On the line, up the line."** We want to be several steps up, feet in front. We always talk to post players about their feet.

When the ball is at the **wing**, we will always play **baseline side**. If the wing gets beat on the baseline side, I want the post to help. If the post is on the highside and the wing gets beat, there is no help. As far as defending the post, it is easier for weakside help to get to the highside than it is for weakside help to get to the lowside.

How do you get to the lowside? Your post can go underneath, but she must stay away from the offensive post. You must step away to come around. Don't let the offensive player get her body into you. You can go over the top by stepping through with the near foot. Another way is to go **"arm bar"** over the top. You can do two arm bars and you can get around in front. Now, if the ball is reversed when you are on the lowside, you must go behind. Do not go over the top. Step away and go low. The post players must move their feet.

Weakside Guard

When the ball is one pass away, you must be in a **closed stance** because we **deny** the ball. This is hard to teach. We want the player to be halfway between the man and the ball. If the other guard drives, help and recover. If she is two passes away, open up and drop deeper into the lane. Every time the ball moves, she must move. Don't let your player come to the ball.

Weakside Wing

When the wing is two passes away, **open up** and have one foot in the lane. Deny the **flash cut.** No one catches the ball in the lane. Point at both man and ball; see both.

If the ball is in the post, **double-down.** You also help with a lob pass into the post. If the ball is three passes away, sag into the middle of the lane. Adjust depending on scouting report. If a player can't shoot, we may sag off of her and help inside.

(Diagram 1) We will give up the high-post area before we give up the low-post area. If all three of these players can shoot, you are in trouble anyway.

(Diagram 2) On the **screen across**. When X2 is screened, X2 finds the screen with her back and then slides with the girl coming off of the screen. X2 should be in weakside help so it should be hard to screen X2. On the perimeter, we switch all screens.

Now for some drills. We spend a lot of time, especially with the JV team, walking. We talk about **sliding** and keeping the **feet apart**. We want the head to remain at the same level, don't bounce. We used to do group slides, and when I pointed, the players would move three slides in one direction. Now, we move two steps in one direction, and then the third slide would be in the opposite direction. This step must be taken with the lead foot. The legs are always spread.

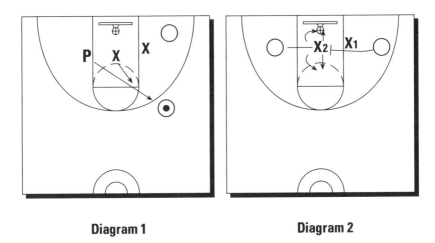

Diagram 1	Diagram 2

(Diagram 3) **The Corner Drill.** Use a cone, have the dribbler try to get out of the corner. The defensive players must slide and cut off the dribbler. We don't want people to drop-step.

(Diagram 4) **Deny the pass to the wing.** After the wing gets the ball, the defensive wing must get her half-step advantage to the baseline.

(Diagram 5) **One-on-one.** Don't let the dribbler get into the lane. I want a block or a charge. Don't open up and escort her in for a layup.

Diagram 3   **Diagram 4**

Diagram 5

(Diagram 6) **Weakside Defense.** The dribbler will move up and down with the ball. The defensive player must constantly be moving, and she must not let her player flash to the ball. If she goes above the free-throw line, that's fine. If she makes a backdoor cut, don't lose the player.

(Diagram 7) **Combination Drills.** Deny the wing pass. If the wing gets the pass, get into a good defensive position. The wing then passes the ball back to the coach. The coach will either pass the ball back to the wing again or else will pass the ball to the weakside. If the ball is passed to the weakside, then the defensive player must deny the flash cut into the lane.

(Diagram 8) **Two-on-two drill** with the coach as the passer. Defensive players must react to deny the wing defense on the strongside and deny the flash cut from the weakside. No shots, constantly pass.

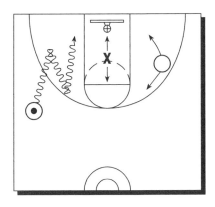

Diagram 6   **Diagram 7**

Diagram 8

Chapter Six

BUILDING A TEAM DEFENSE

Jeff Jones

Playing hard on defense is enough to reach success. You must teach and ground your players in the techniques of defense. We want to play great, hard-nosed defense and **contest** every shot. In the ACC this year, we were the #1 defensive team. Even though we were one of the smallest teams in our league, we were third in rebounding. Building your team defense is no different from any other type of construction. You start with a strong foundation and gradually add to it until you have the finished product.

The foundation of your team defense is built through fundamentals and basic defensive principles. At the University of Virginia, we try to reinforce those principles beginning with the very first day of practice. We begin by working on individual defensive drills, then progressing to two-man, four-man, and finally five-man defensive situations. We believe strongly in first learning **proper defensive techniques** before going live. This is where teaching enters the picture. Once we go **"live,"** our coach's role is more motivating, encouraging, and correcting of mistakes. While we have an idea about how quickly we would like to progress, it is important not to rush or skip any fundamentals.

Like any building project, this will show up as a weakness at some point. There are several important keys to playing good individual and team defense. They are as follows: **Communication, Desire, Enthusiasm, Unselfishness,** and **an Understanding of What Is Expected.**

Before we start talking about the drills we use to teach our defense, I would like to take time to look at the key terminology and concepts/ philosophy we build our defense around.

TERMINOLOGY

Stay Flat—contain dribbler. We don't **force** the ball sideline or middle. We keep our feet parallel to the offensive player and stay between the ball and the basket. Don't **bail out** the shooter. We don't want to foul the shooter. We **contest** every shot, but we don't foul. We don't want to put people at the free throw line.

Trail/fight through. We follow the same path on cutters away from the ball. We don't like to fight through screens so we **trail** and show **help** from the defender on the screener. We have the man who is guarding the screener give the appearance of coming off his man to pick up the cutter.

Jump to the ball. We don't stand still on the pass; we move as the ball is in the air.

Front/strong straddle/behind. These are the basic ways we could **defend the post.** We like the second choice. We place our highside arm in the passing lane, our back forearm is on the hip of the offensive post, our back foot is locked on the inside of the offensive post's upper foot.

Flex/dig it out/stay. These are the choices you have in adjusting to passes going into the post. We stress the **dig.** We have our guard/forward go halfway to help on the post, but we don't **deny** the pass back out. If the post would put the ball on the floor, we would **double down.**

Close/open/neutral or parallel/swivel. These are the different stances we use in guarding the ball and dribbler. In the **close position,** we are in a **denial stance.** However, we only place the up hand in the passing lane, not the body. We only deny a step beyond the three-point line.

CONCEPTS/PHILOSOPHY

The things we stress in our team defensive philosophy are:

- **No penetration**—We don't allow this either by the pass or the dribble. We work extremely hard defending the dribbler. We do this because the **dribble is the weakness** at all levels of play. Learning to do this eases the burden of help and recover.

- **Position defense**

- **Rebounding position**

- **Stay between the man and the basket**—allow no backdoors

- **Hand in passing lane,** not body

- **Mental discipline**—patience— When you hear the word patience, you think of offense more than defense. You know that if you can make a team play defense longer than 20-25 seconds, they start to loose their concentration. Because of this, we practice making our team play defense from 30-35 seconds so they learn to be patient and mentally tough.

Before the season begins, we cover specific **defensive situations.** It is important that you have the answers for these situations before they arise. The defensive situations we cover are:

–How hard to play on the ball

–How to play "off the ball" (perimeter)

–How to play in the low post

–How to defend the "post-to-post" screens

–How to defend a man coming "off a downscreen" away from the ball

–How to guard the "man setting the downscreen"

–How to defend ball screens

-When and from where do you doubleteam the low post

-How to close out on a man

-How to defend shuffle cuts

-How to defend 2-on-1 transition

-How to defend the UCLA dive cut

The drills we use to teach our defense are:

- **Stance and slide**

(Diagram 1) We do this drill every day during the first week of practice for 10 minutes. We will only do it after this as a refresher. The players line up in lines of four or five. The coach says **stance** and the players get down with one foot slightly in front of the other. On the whistle, they step and slide; on the next whistle, they step and slide coming back the other way with the opposite foot forward. We will always open and slide in this drill. Stress throwing the elbow in the direction you're turning so you get open quickly.

Diagram 1

- **One-on-one drill**—do this from various areas of the floor and we go full court, half-court, or quarter-court.

- **Zigzag drill**

- **Defensive slide and communication**

(Diagram 2) The whole squad forms one line under the basket. Each player in a **defensive stance** slides to half-court, back to the foul line, over to the right sideline, and then all the way back across the floor to the left sideline. The next player starts as the player immediately in front of him reaches the foul line.

- **Man in the middle**

(Diagram 3) This is just plain three-man **keep-away**. Each player spends a minute in the middle.

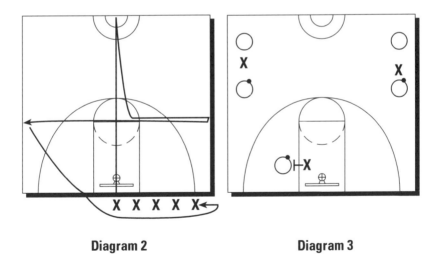

Diagram 2   Diagram 3

- ## One-on-one checkout and rebound

(Diagram 4) We have an offensive player and defensive player line up on the foul line. A coach/manager at the wing shoots the ball. The defender must make **contact, seal, and recover the ball**.

- ## Defend the dive cut and flash drill

(Diagram 5) The drill begins with an offensive and defensive player at the guard position. The offensive guard passes to the coach/manager at the wing, starts away and tries to **face cut** coming back to the ball.

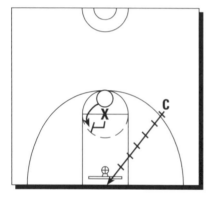

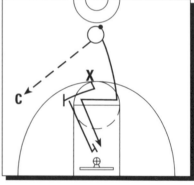

Diagram 4　　　　　　　**Diagram 5**

(Diagram 6) The defender must **jump to the ball,** force the offense behind him on the cut, staying below the ball so the offense cannot get a layup. The offensive player continues through the lane to the weakside. The defender must stop in help position, seeing man and ball.

(Diagram 7) You need to really stress this because most players tend to follow their man all the way through the lane. To emphasize this, the coach/manager could dribble to the basket, forcing the helpside defender to stop the dribbler before he gets in the lane. The offensive player, after cutting to the weakside of the floor, executes a **flash cut** to the high post. The defender must now deny the flash to the three-point line extended. If the offensive player gets the ball, we go one-on-one live, and on the shot, we check out and rebound.

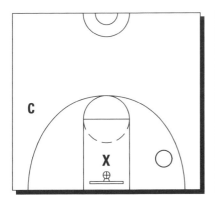 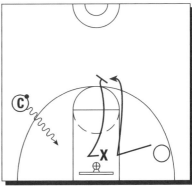

Diagram 6   **Diagram 7**

- **Deny the wing**

(Diagram 8) The drill starts with an offensive and defensive man in the wing position. The offensive player makes a pass out to the coach/manager and cuts to basket. The defender gets a hand, not the body, in the passing lane. As the offensive player makes a **backdoor cut,** the defender turns, but does not open to the ball. As the offensive player cuts through the lane, the coach/manager **reverses the ball,** and we play one-on-one denial on the opposite side.

- **Work around the post drill**

(Diagram 9) We do this on both sides of the floor. The ball starts in the corner on one side and on the top on the other. On a pass from the top to the corner, the defensive post brings his foot up and over the top of the offensive post. We are now fronting the post, with hands up, and leaning on the offensive player so we can feel him. On the pass from the corner to the top, our post is to **go behind,** not over the **top** of the post.

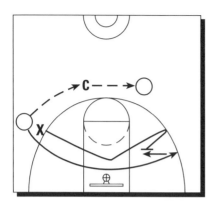

Diagram 8

Diagram 9

- **Two-on-two help and recover**

(Diagram 10) Guard-to-guard

(Diagram 11) Guard-to-forward or forward-to-guard

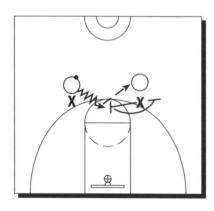

Diagram 10

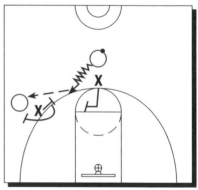

Diagram 11

- **Defend screens off the ball**

(Diagram 12) We work on two things on this drill: we fight **through** the screen and get **square.**

(Diagram 13) We work on trailing and getting square.

 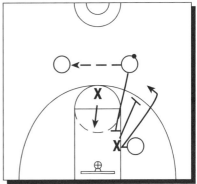

Diagram 12   **Diagram 13**

- **3-on-3/4-on-4 transition**

(Diagram 14) We line three or four men up on the baseline with a defender at the foul line extended facing them. The coach is at the top of the key with a ball. He passes to one of the men on the baseline. The defender whose man receives the pass must run and touch the baseline before he can get back defensively. The coach can tell the offensive players they must make so many passes before shooting. He can also state that a certain offensive player must score.

- **Three-man stance and slide/return 2-on-1**

(Diagram 15) Three players line up on the foul line extended facing the coach who is under the basket. On his signal, they begin to shuffle and slide toward half-court. The coach throws a ball to one of the three defenders, who takes the ball hard to the basket. The other two defenders must get back and stop the drive.

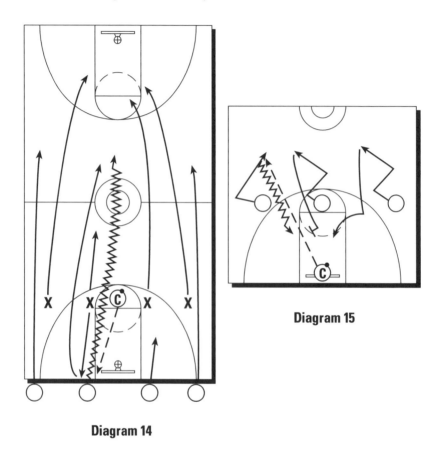

Diagram 15

Diagram 14

- **Shell drill**—here we work on different situations.

(Diagram 16) **Baseline breakdown**—The man who gets beaten on the baseline drive must come all the way across the lane and pick up the man on the opposite baseline. When he gets there, he pushes the weakside guard back up to pick up his man.

(Diagram 17) **Weakside exchange**—The guard with the ball makes a pass to the forward on his side. The offside guard and forward execute a weakside exchange. On the guard-to-forward pass, we stress the guard whose man goes to the baseline must move down the lane to helpside position and not to move to guard his man.

(Diagram 18) **Guard dive and rotate**—Here the guard makes a pass to the forward and cuts to the basket. We are working on the fundamentals we taught in the dive-cut drill. We don't allow our cutter to post up.

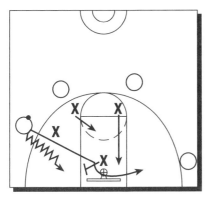

Diagram 16

Diagram 17

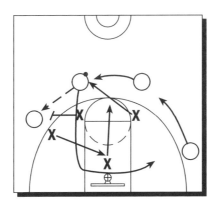

Diagram 18

(Diagram 19) **Clearout and replace**—Here the guard drives at the forward signaling a **clearout.** The offensive forward cuts across the lane to the weakside position and the weakside guard, and forward rotates toward the ball. We want the defenders moving to the weakside to stop in the lane, open up, see the man and ball, not follow his man all the way through.

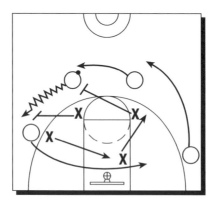

Diagram 19

- **Five-on-five.** Our basic half-court defense is what we call our **Blue Coverage.** In this defense, we extend ourselves to approximately the three-point line and do not contest any perimeter passes from beyond this point. We will contest penetrating passes inside the three-point area at all times—that is, passes into the lane or toward the basket. Although we are not really trying to take a team out of their offense, we will play very tough and physical in a confined area.

Starting penetration dribbles or passes inside the three-point arc is the starting point of this defense, and rebounding the ball (after only one shot attempt) is the finishing point.

Chapter Seven

TEACHING MAN-TO-MAN DEFENSE

Brian Mahoney

In teaching defense, you must develop a great pride in stopping the other team. This must start from the very first day of practice. The basic keys to defense as we see it at St. John's are:

- **Pressure on the ball.** We pick people up at the **"door."** This means we pick people up three feet outside the NBA three-point line.

- **Make the next pass difficult.** Force a player high and wide to get the pass.

- **Helpside defense.** When away from the ball, get in the lane to give help. Players must learn to contain the dribble. We don't want the ball in the middle third of the court. We funnel everything to the sideline. Once the ball goes below the foul line extended, we **force** the ball to the **baseline.** We don't want to give up easy baskets, especially on transition defense. We want to hold the opponent to one shot. We emphasize our guards should rebound as well as the big men.

DRILLS WE USE TO TEACH DEFENSE ARE:

(Diagram 1) **1-on-1 full-court defense.** The defense passes to the offense to start the drill and then sprints to half-court. He then turns and picks up the offensive player, forcing him away from the basket.

(Diagram 2) **3-on-3 full-court defense.** The coach throws the ball to the offense who is lined up on the baseline. The defense sprints to half-court and then turns and picks up the ball. The two defenders whose men don't have the ball must sprint back below the line of the ball and stop any penetration. We call this **"building a wall."**

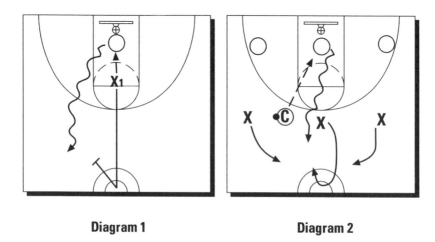

Diagram 1   **Diagram 2**

(Diagram 3) **4-on-4 full-court defense.** This is the same as the 3-on-3 drill with another offensive and defensive player added. The responsibilities are the same for the defenders. To make this drill more difficult, you can change who the defense is guarding so they can't just sprint back and pick up a man. They might have to change sides of the court to pick their man up.

(Diagram 4) **Contest the shot.** This is a drill of three defensive players versus four offensive players. We allow no dribbling, just passing by the offense. We allow only jump shots at first, and then we allow baseline offensive drives. The defense stays on defense until they get the rebound.

We run a shell drill to work on several things:

- **Defend the Pass and Cut** (Diagram 5). We tell our defenders to jump to the ball and front the cutter. The offense rotates on the pass and cut.

Diagram 3

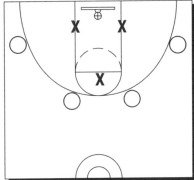

Diagram 4

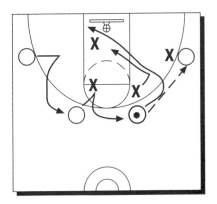

Diagram 5

- **Defend the Downscreen** (Diagram 6). The man on the ball must pressure the ball. The man being screened has the right of way to get through and get to the ball. We encourage his teammates to pull him through the screen.

- **Help and Recover.** (Diagram 7). The offense now looks to drive when they get the ball. Emphasis is on the defense stopping the penetrating dribble.

Diagram 6   **Diagram 7**

(Diagram 8) **"Diamond" Drill.** Every third pass must go to the post. We are emphasizing the defender on the outside **"digging down"** on the pass to the post and then getting back out to the pick-up man. The offense can pass, cut, screen, etc. We encourage a skip-pass and drive to force the defense to have to recover and stop the drive.

Diagram 8

(Diagram 9) **"Spit Out" Drill.** This is a four-on-five drill in which we have an open post. The post, however, can only catch the ball on the block. Every third pass must go to the post. The offense can make any cut they want. We run all these drills four to five minutes every day. If a drill isn't going well, we'll go on to the next drill and then come back to it later.

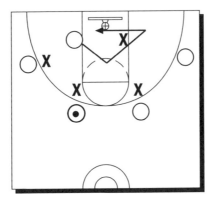

Diagram 9

Chapter Eight

UTAH DEFENSE

Rick Majerus

The first thing you must decide on defense is how many men you are going to have back. We always drop two men back. Next year, I am considering dropping only one man back with a certain lineup. We always keep two men back (our guards) because we feel that if you have a guard who will get two or three rebounds a game, you have a very good rebounder. But he would probably have to score two of those three to justify not giving up any fast breaks. We don't want to give up easy baskets. We drop our point guard to half-court and our 2 guard to the basket. We try to establish a **driving line.** We think the most important thing in transition defense is to not give up the **easy basket.** We want the ball out of the middle of the floor. Everything we do defensively is predicated on getting the ball out of the middle of the floor. We want the ball **pushed to the sideline** and get a driving line.

I spent some time with Don Nelson, who is probably better than any coach in basketball. I really believe him to be the best. Nellie always looked at a player to see what he **could do**, not what he **couldn't do.** He would put his players in positions where they could do what they did best, especially with big men. When I recruit a big man, I ask him where his favorite spot is. Often he will say that he is good on both blocks. This usually means that he is equally bad on both sides. The great players of the game always have a favorite side of the floor. Karl Malone likes the left block. Kareem wanted the left block.

I took Nellie's philosophy and put players in situations defensively where they could excel. Some are best at not being screened, so I would not play that man on the point guard. We want our 3, 4, and 5 men back in a certain time. If they don't make it, we sprint. We do not **trace the ball** on defense. There is a good argument to be made either way, for tracing the rebounder and jamming the pass. I believe in the **body game,** and we do a lot with the **weakside seal.** We don't have a lot of jumpers. **We teach getting into the body and making contact.** This is done with a **reverse pivot and sealing** the defensive player under the basket. He doesn't have to worry about jumping. We would rather have him concentrate on getting the pivot and seal than tracing the ball after the other team gets the rebound. We get two men back. We call them the fullback, the halfback, and the others are tailbacks. One player is all the way back, one is halfway back, and the others have to get their tails back.

One thing we do in conversion...we want to talk, and point...but we convert back to a side of the floor. We want the ball pushed to the side, and we want everybody to get to that side. We pay particular attention to **closing out the wings.** We don't want to close out from the paint to the wing because you get beat on the dribble. There are only two things we do every day. We really do this every day. One is that we do **skill development** every day. We go from 12 minutes to an hour daily to develop players. You can develop players with skill development. We do dribbling, passing, and shooting every day. This is a game of skill. The second thing we do every day is **conversion defense.** That's how important we thought it was. We felt our defense began with stopping the break. We didn't want to give up easy layups. We scouted a lot. We put an inordinate amount of time in scouting. We played everybody differently. If you have great talent, I would always play pressure defense. When your talent is not equal, we played scouting report defense. We do have some rules. First, above the 28-foot mark, we try to force everything to the sideline. Below, we either push to the sideline or baseline. We will change this depending on our opponent, but we always have a definite push so everyone knows where the help is coming from.

How you play the swing of the ball, the ball reversal, is correlated with how you play your forwards.

(Diagram 1) If the ball is on the wing, and we **push** baseline or sideline, then we are **denying** the reversal of the ball.

(Diagram 2) However, if we are **pushing middle**, then we do not deny because there is **no help.** So we play **soft.** How you play the swing of the ball is predicated on how you play the ball on the wing.

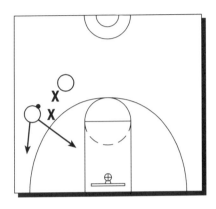

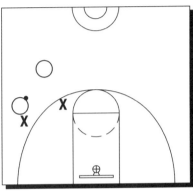

Diagram 1   Diagram 2

The next thing we do is **switch** everything we can. We switch everything of our equal size. We have four rules: **talk it, touch it, switch it, deny it.** We **talk the switch,** especially on back picks. It is important for your team to realize that the backpicker is the important man calling the switch. Second, **we touch it.** The two players switching come together and touch. We over touch with an arm from each player extended to the shoulder of the other player. We don't want them to split this. We then **switch** and **deny.** There is no sense in switching if you don't deny. We like to **switch small out, big in.** I don't know how much contact you can get away with at the high school level, but we **body** players. Next, we try to **deny the ball** at the elbow. We don't want the ball at the elbow and then we don't allow the high-post to low-post pass. We play the post about as many ways as you can play the post. Unless the high post is a great catch and shoot player, we don't deny the high-post pass. We usually let the big man catch it high. We align our inside shoulder up with the outside shoulder and are about two steps back. This takes away the backdoor pass. We want active hands. We have our hands up head high. We want a hand up on every shot. If he goes to **turn and shoot,** we already have our hands up. Anytime a player moves from high post to low post, we always disrupt route and timing. We never let a player move down the lane without **physical contact.** He must either go outside me or inside me. If we are going to play behind, one-quarter front or side front, we **bump him outside.** If we are going to play three-quarter front or full front, we **bump him inside.** We want to distort timing and route. We try to play defense body to body, bumping him from behind with our body and bumping him out of his preferred position. You must body them out inch by inch. There is a real subtlety to this. Keep your hands high, and this draws attention to the fact that we aren't fouling. Now, I said we don't allow the high-post pass. This is the only exception, to the big man. Remember, we never play everybody the same. We scout, look at personnel, and then we decide. When they feed the high post, and then the high post turns, we get right up on him so that he must try to drive.

(Diagram 3) This is what I mean by driving line. We want to keep the ball out of the middle. We try to bump every curl with the man who is defending the screener. The best way to beat the screen is the **slash,** where you just fight through it. But in high school and college, they call that. It is very hard to body your way through a screen. So, there are two other ways to do it. As my man goes to set a screen, I try to keep my nose in his chest or my ear in his chest. My teammate will get on the hip of the man who is to be screened. This is a **downscreen** from the wing to the block. I get in the way of the man coming off the screen and take the hit. I bump the curl, distorting route and timing. On every lob, we try to go to the body. Very few people understand that is the way to play the lob. We squeeze the man as tightly as we can. We go to the body and jump. As I come down with the screener, I throw an arm, keep vision on the ball, and I have 3/4 of my body in line with the screener. There is no question that I am **vulnerable** to the step-up. But we think that this step-up is like a backdoor. We don't concern ourselves when a player makes a tough play and gets a backdoor. So more than likely, they will curl. We bump the curl and distort route and timing.

(Diagram 4) We do this on single, double screens. We try to send them off the single side, but it is always a personnel decision. The ball is at the elbow. 3 can go either way. Our first choice is to **switch.** The second choice is to go with the **body and bump the curl.**

(Diagram 5) If it is a **seal double,** invert it. 1 has the ball. X3 will move to the top of the stack. As 2 comes off the screen, X3 will take 2, X2 will take 3.

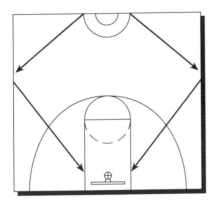

Diagram 3

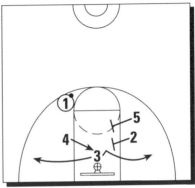

Diagram 4

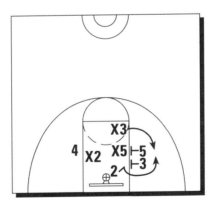

Diagram 5

(Diagram 6) **Triangle action** is hard to defend. Anytime you have a small on big, **cross screen** with a down screen. 2 picks 5. 4 then picks 2. X3 will switch on 2, X2 will take 3. This is also called an **invert.** This stuff is tough to teach, but if you can get your players started early in junior high and get the coaches there to teach the same things that you teach with the same terminology, then you have a chance to be successful.

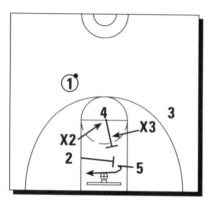

Diagram 6

You must be in charge of the entire program. More than anything, if I were a high school coach, I would want to **control** my under coaches. Not that I wouldn't give them any freedom, that's not the right way either. I not only listen to my assistant coaches, but I listen to my players. If a player has a suggestion, I will almost always go with it. Number one, they will work like heck to make it work. Number two, they are out there playing, and I'm not. Number three, I always want them thinking the game of basketball and I invite their opinions. Maybe you can't do this in high school because of the age of the kids. But, I think that if you give the kids responsibility, it will be to your advantage.

Let's get back to defending the post. We either front, 3/4, 1/2, play behind or push out, and sometimes we **circle.** We never let the post move where he wants to go without making some attempt to distort route and timing. Take the low post. The first thing is to beat your man to the spot, then bump him out or bump him in. We will try to inch you out. "Inch by inch it is a cinch." Everyone in America has a preferential shoulder. We scout ourselves silly. We look at films "ad nauseam." If you tell me that you have a player who doesn't have a preferential shoulder, then you have a terrific player. Each man has his favorite move. We get to a shoulder and make them go the other way. We **gap** the catch and play the shoulder with high and active hands. If he is going to **drop step,** we want him to come through our body. Get the charge. If there is a great size difference, on the swing of the ball from the side to the top when you are in a 3/4 front, we then **side the post**. We get on the side and put an arm across him and lock our thigh with his and body him. If you are going to invite the lob, then you must be pressuring the passer. If you have a double size disadvantage, you can't stop the pass. We also **circle the post.** We keep a gap and keep them guessing. We don't want them to find our body. So, beat the player down the floor, move him off the spot, and distort route and timing. Then you must play according to your personnel vs. his. Know his preferential shoulder and his go-to-it move. Where does your help come from?

Sometimes we cover down from the perimeter. Sometimes we cover from the feeder. We either come on the catch, on the first bounce or on the second bounce. But everybody is always in a **drop.** A drop means that you open sideways, halfway to the post. We keep vision on the ball and vision on the man. If I am not in a cover down off of a catch or a dribble, I am in a drop. We come off of the second dribble on everybody. So, we drop on post feed and come on the second dribble off of everybody. Some players we come on the catch or the first bounce. Depends on the scouting report. Whenever we come to double the post, we come big with active hands. We come on an inside angle and we always **seal** the middle. We travel on the air time of the ball. That's one of our cardinal rules; travel on the air time of the ball. We show players on the film when they don't do it. On a **skip-pass,** you must close out on the air time of the ball. When they come down to double the post, I would rather they come on a semicircular route than straight. If he comes straight, the post can split the double. If he comes on the bowed route, he is closer to the basket and in better defensive position.

Another way is to **dive.** When you are against a great post player, you turn and dive into the post, get a hand in the post. We also go 60/40, 50/50; we fake and fade with active hands in the post. We believe that there are very few players who can shoot out of rhythm. When I was with Nellie, at that point, he felt that there were only 13 players in the NBA who could shoot out of rhythm. You are talking about the greatest players in the greatest league. But just 13. Those are the only players he would concern himself with by going soft on the wing. We would fake and fade with active hands. You must take up space, keeping your back to either the sideline or endline, fake and fade with high and active hands. You are always ready to get your hand up on the shooter. Not into the shooter, but **vertically up.** We stress that. If you have a player who is a wide body, teach him to take a charge. Now you have forced the bounce pass.

(Diagram 7) We want all of our charges taken outside of the lane. We deny the nearest man. The man who is two passes away will rotate down. The man taking the charge goes right above the block outside the lane. We take away the bounce pass. Take decisions away from your players. We want them to attack penetration.

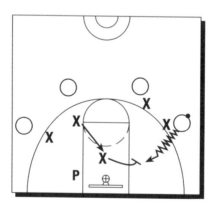

Diagram 7

You never err with an aggressive foul. Establish an aggressive mind-set. The toughest thing to do is to alter the personality of someone. The toughest thing you are going to have with most big men is to get them aggressive. They haven't had to be. Big players aren't aggressive because of their mothers. The world's expectations for big players is for them to be tough. The world sees this kid as more advanced than he is. So his mother protects him. As a coach, you must nurture and foster that.

Let's talk about the **cross screen.** We look to switch. The toughest pick for a big man to get around is a small player. He gets into their legs; he has a lower, wider base. We try to use small/big cross screens. Then we take away the low cut and bump high. We play the cross screen high/high, high/low, low/high, low/low. We will play it as many ways as there are. Everything we do is predicated on their personnel vs. ours and what that team is trying to do.

(Diagram 8) This is a small/big cross screen and we are going to play it high/high. The first thing we do is take away the low cut. We want B (big) to come over the top. He will get bumped and he is farther from the basket. If the ball is shot when this is going on, we are in a better rebounding position. S (small) must **bump the cutter.** Small man has four jobs. He must defend the post initially, talk and call the cross screen, bump the cutter, and see the man through. The man whose man is receiving the cross screen must body his man up, go over the screen, and take away the low cut. Is this hard? Yes. Do we do a lot on defense? Yes. We spend an hour a day on defense so that when we go into a game, we know how we are playing the picks, how we are playing the back-pick, the cross-pick, the pick-and-roll, how we are going to play the post feed, and it varies from game to game.

When the talent is equal, I don't think that you can cover it just one way. If there is one thing that you must come away with here, it is a philosophy of what you have. How are you going to play these things? How do you play the wing? Here is a teaching point: You will have a good low stance if you have either the ear in chest or the nose in chest. If a man makes a flash cut, we take him on **diagonally** and take him on with ear in chest. We want to get into his body, ride him out or make him go backdoor. On the wing, most of the time we play soft. We deny him out as far as we can. We always point our toe on the denial. That's a good teaching point.

(Diagram 9) You will be a lot quicker if you can point the toe out. Plus your body is turned and you see the ball better.

After the wing catches the ball, we **go soft on the wing.** If he is a good shooter, we won't go soft. We usually gap him about one man away. If we are soft on the wing, and we are pushing to the sideline or the baseline (remember we are denying the reversal of the ball), we think it is harder to feed the post and we won't get beat on the dribble. To feed the post, you must take the ball to the defender. We are encouraging him to put the ball on the floor, but only if he is not a good shooter. We play some straight up, some we force left, some we make dribble. We do a lot of things. When I played, I was a bad player and I knew I was a bad player. When the ball came to me and I was open, I didn't want to shoot anyway and when they backed off of me, it really put the pressure on. It's hard for kids to hit those shots. If I was a high school coach, I would never let the other team's star beat me. Let's say that this is the star. We would never let him beat us down the stretch.

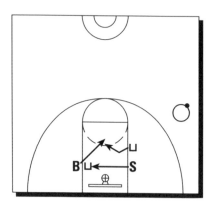

Diagram 8

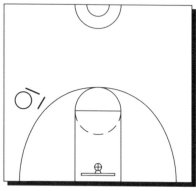

Diagram 9

(Diagram 10) We could **double** him. Here's our angle, and we double him. We come on a curved route. We hope that he takes on the double. We would force him to his left. If he did pass out and go on a weakside cut, never send your double-team player with him. Don't ask the perimeter man who is running in one direction to turn and go in the other.

(Diagram 11) The **post** is the star. The letters are on defense. Anytime we double in the post with A and B, C and D are guarding three men.

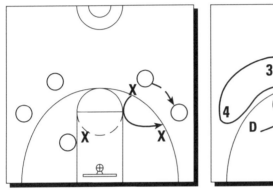

Diagram 10

Diagram 11

(Diagram 12) When the ball comes out of the post, we send B weak to pick up.

(Diagram 13) If the ball is passed out on the weakside, D will pick up high and B will cover low. Any double into the post we go weak and pick up.

At the high school level, don't let the star beat you. There aren't that many good players on one team. Even if you have three good players, there is still a pecking order with one better than the others. I wouldn't do this every time. I would vary it. Let me tell you what we did. We got all of our team in a room and asked them who was the greatest player in the game. Nine out of 12 named Jordan. We got them to all agree that if Jordan wasn't the greatest, he was one of the greatest. We said that you can all do what Jordan does. We showed them Jordan taking four charges, diving on the floor for loose balls, hustling back on defense. We showed them Jordan leading the break, but when Pippen yells, **"through,"** Jordan goes 100 miles an hour and takes the defense with him, and Pippen fills the spot for the jumper. We said, "Here's Jordan. Want to be like Jordan? Take a charge, dive for the loose ball, run back on defense. Hustle your tail off. You can do that."

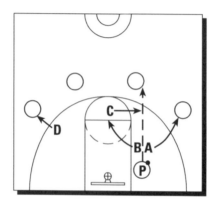

Diagram 12

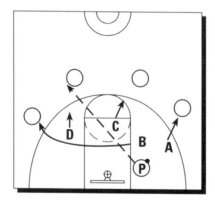

Diagram 13

Chapter Nine

LONGHORN DEFENSE

Tom Penders

We number our man offenses with **10** being **full-court. 7** is **3/4 court. 5** is **half-court. 3** is the **three-point area.** Our traps: **99** is **full-court trap, 77** is **3/4, 55** is **half-court, 33** is from the **three-point line.** Late in the game, if we are ahead, we play it straight. We do no trapping; we switch all screens, and we don't want to give the three-point shots. I would say that 90 percent of the time we played some form of man-to-man **trap** and **rotate** this year. When we would trap depended on our scouting report.

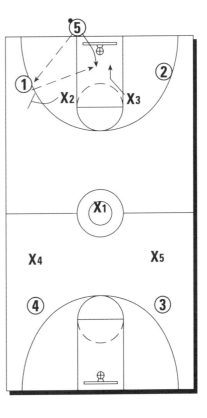

(Diagram 1) **21 Match-tip Press.** This is a 2-1-2. X1 is our quickest defender. We are looking to trap the dribbler. Suppose 5 inbounds the ball to 1. X2 takes 1. X3 is matched up with 2, but plays as if it's a man-to-man press. He has **ball, you, man responsibility.** If there is no one in the middle, X1 will match up with 5. However, when the ball is reversed to 5 in this type of situation, we don't **double** 5 because he will be able to throw over the trap. We leave him all alone. It is an automatic.

Diagram 1

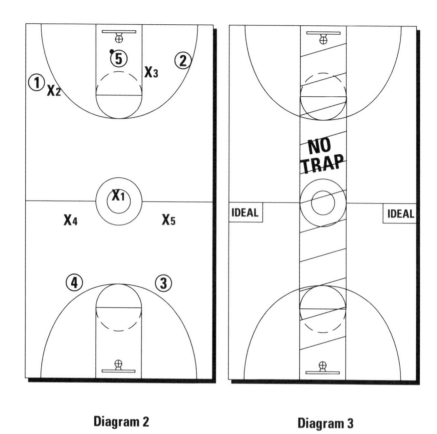

Diagram 2   **Diagram 3**

(Diagram 2) 5, the center, who is not a good dribbler, has the ball by himself. We are **denying everything.** As 5 starts dribbling, X1 starts closing down.

(Diagram 3) We **never trap** in the middle. We like to trap on the sideline. The ideal place is just over half-court on the sideline.

(Diagram 4) If the ball is being dribbled up the side, X 2 stays with him, and X1 comes over and traps with X2.

(Diagram 5) X1 cannot come over to make that **trap;** X4 will come up and set the trap with X2. X5 comes over to ballside as X1 drops deep.

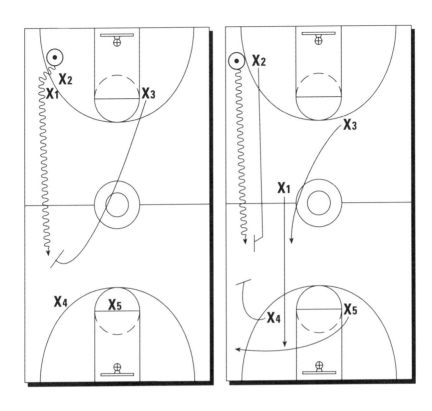

Diagram 4   **Diagram 5**

(Diagram 6) If they **throw out of the trap,** X4, who got beat, turns and follows and traps with X1. X5 drops, as do X2 and X3. Scouting is important.

(Diagram 7) **Doubling-down** on the center is important. Again, scouting is important. Suppose 2 is the weakest shot on the offense. If 1 passes to 5, X2 rotates over and guards 4, and X4 drops down to help with 5. X3 sags into the lane. If 1 couldn't shoot, X1 would double-down. So, you must change from game to game. Offensively, your worst shooter must come and get the ball and **swing** it to his teammate.

(Diagram 8) We **trap all ballscreens.** We don't want him open to shoot the three. We feel that this is an opportunity for the steal.

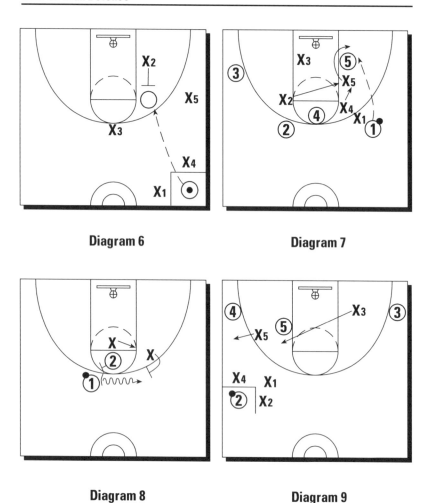

Diagram 6   Diagram 7

Diagram 8   Diagram 9

(Diagram 9) When in doubt, **trap.** We leave the man open farthest from the ball. X3 is moving in to cover 5 as X5 moves out to the side.

(Diagram 10) If a **trap is beaten** in the back-court, and the pass is made to mid-court, our rule is to sprint to the line of the ball. One man comes up to cover the receiver, but we do not trap there. We never run from one trap to another. Nobody is that quick. Everyone is looking to help each other. You have five players working together.

(Diagram 11) We played Temple this year, and they used a **stack** offense. They brought 3 around the stack out to the wing. We trapped their dribbler with our X1 and X4 and brought X5 across the lane to help.

Diagram 11

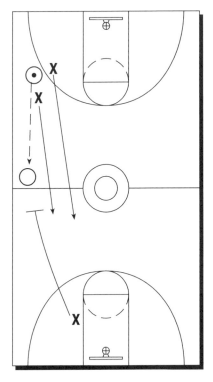

Diagram 10

Chapter Ten

BEARS DEFENSE

Charlie Spoonhour

There are three things that are important once you get on the floor. Basically, they all involve defense. When we took the job at Southwest Missouri, we had short players and were concerned because we had to play people who were better and we asked what we could do to win games. Your job is not to outsmart anybody. Your job is to be smart enough to control your kids and give them a chance to win. That is your job. At any level, if you do three or four things defensively, you will have a chance to win. What I am going to talk about will lead up to these three things.

You are going to **stop fast breaks and the easy layups.** You are going to **contest shots,** and you are going to rebound the ball and **not foul.** One of the worst things that ever happened to us was when Al McGuire used to talk about having fouls to waste. I was with Hubie Brown for a week, and I think Hubie is one of the most intelligent men in the game. He said if you foul a shooter, you have lost your mind. **Never foul a shooter.** The only possible time is on a layup. The percentages turn so much in favor of the offensive player when you foul. When you foul a shooter, you are taking anywhere from a 39 percent to a 49 percent shooter and you put him on the foul line where he works at about 75 percent or 80 percent. It's simple mathematics.

The first thing you are going to do is to stop the other team from shooting layups. This shouldn't be difficult, but it is. When I first started, I had no organization in terms of getting back defensively. I just yelled, "Why are they shooting layups?" and no one knew the answer, including me.

The answer was that my team was disorganized. Your team is the most disorganized when you shoot and miss a shot or when you turn the ball over. Watch your team run down the floor after a missed shot or a turnover. They will trot. You must get your team to **sprint** down the floor defensively. You must get them organized.

(Diagram 1) We have two players whom we assign back. That is their job, they **do not rebound.** We used to say whoever is at the head of the circle is back. Well, that doesn't work. Take the excuses out of the game. We assign two to get back. One goes to the middle of the floor; we try to put our point guard there because most teams are going to run breaks by getting the ball to their point guard. We take our worst rebounder and we run him to the goal. This may not be a guard. The deep man protects the goal, he keeps the other team from shooting a layup. Don't tell him just to get back. He may go anywhere. Tell him to get back until he is in the shade of the goal. Then he is in the right spot. The man in the middle is not going to take the ball away from the other point guard, nor is he going to stop him dead on the floor. The only thing he is going to do is to slow him down so that your other three players will have a chance to run back. You are buying time for the other three players. We tell the other three that when you see you are not going to get a rebound, run. **Run down the floor.** We do not jam the outlet man. If I tell them to do that, they will foul 84' from the goal, which is insane.

(Diagram 2) If the ball is **shot from the right side, you run back the same way you do offensively.** You turn to the outside and start back. No one runs in the middle except the point guard. As you are running and scan the floor and don't see your man down the floor, obviously, he is behind. I turn and find **ball first, man second.** Common sense will then tell me what to do. We do a good job early in the year doing this. But, if you're not careful as the year goes along, you will quit doing things like this. We do this every day in pre- season, start out 5-on-2. The secret to it is getting players to run and getting them out of the middle of the court.

(Diagram 3) If the other team runs a **sideline break,** the point guard does not go over, he calls **"sideline"** and drops down to the basket. When the point guard touches the hand of the man under, that man goes out. He comes out on baseline side and stops the dribble.

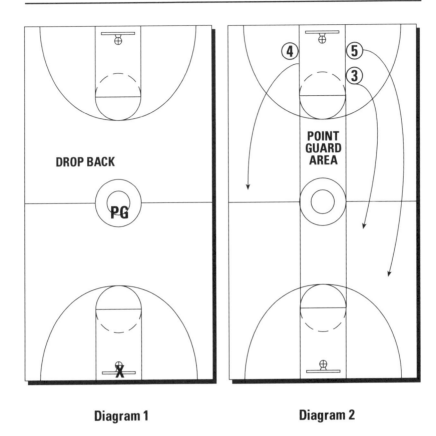

Diagram 1   Diagram 2

(Diagram 4) The only thing we do differently is that the **man on the wing will move with the first pass** as it goes the from wing to the center of the floor. We keep the man under the basket. Theoretically, the other defenders should be back by now anyway. We don't want to leave the basket open. You are probably saying that the man in the middle is going to get some shots. The answer is yes, but what would you rather have, this shot or the shot under the goal? If a team breaks all the time we will drop three people. This comes from scouting. That's what happens on a missed shot.

(Diagram 5) **For turnovers, the rule is to run like the devil.** You know that is one of the hardest things to do. They all want to stand and put their head down. The first player to get to mid-court must yell,

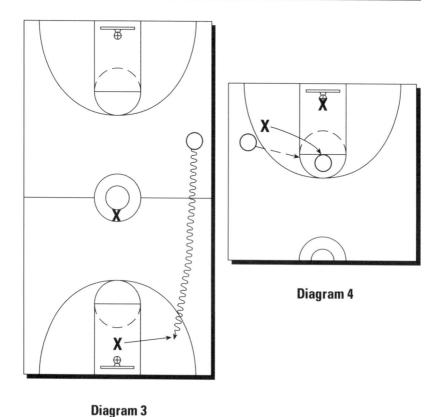

Diagram 4

Diagram 3

"I've got the hole" and he runs under the basket. The next one closest to the ball will attack the ball. The other three run back and find people. We practice this by running motion. I will have an extra ball, pitch it to the defense and yell "turnover." Our players have to **run back.** You must scout and know when your opponents run. You must know the mentality of the people you are playing. When I was a high school coach, I scouted every night. I wasn't married and didn't have much prospect of it. We try to figure out what people are doing. We try to take one or two things out of their offense. If you can do that, you have a good game plan.

Once we are back, here is what we do. Our defense changes every year. You will have the same basic ideas, but will change because of the people you have.

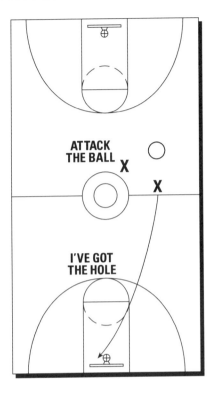

Diagram 5

We play man-to-man defense because it is the easiest thing for me to teach. If you can change defenses and affect the tempo of the game, I think you should do it.

Because we did such a poor job of teaching our zone, we ran **a triangle and two** this year. We also ran it because we had a dwarf playing. If you have a midget and are playing a zone, you have a bad zone. He had little alligator arms that couldn't deflect any balls. We put him man-to-man along with the other guard. Whatever you can teach, do it.

Don't do too much unless you have a great amount of time. If you teach 20 defenses, you will have 20 bad ones. I'd rather have one or two really good ones.

You need to **decide** what you want to do with your man-to-man defense. If you are going to play man defense, you are going to have to work. You are going to have to put out some effort. If you walk out to practice and say, "We're going to overplay the forward, let's go do it," they are not going to overplay him very much. If you don't get out there and get after them, if you are not enthusiastic, you are not going to be able to sell them. Some of you ladies sitting here may think that boys can do that, but girls can't. That's a bunch of bull. Our girls' team guards better than our team. They do every drill we do and do most of them better. I've seen them play. Don't be afraid to demand that they do it. Get some people who are dedicated to what you are trying to do.

We are going to **force** you out of the middle of the floor and keep the **maximum** amount of **pressure** on you. It's a simple thing. Look at yourselves in this room. Most of you have some space between you. You have a little comfort zone. Everyone has a little comfort zone. That's when a basketball player is most comfortable. If you let a player stand, pass, and shoot without you being close enough to bother him, then you aren't really guarding him. You must pressure, and try to dominate your man.

We have changed our feet in our defensive stance. We have a **toe-instep** relationship. We are not parallel. If your feet get parallel, you get beat. We get into the offense a little more. When we had the back foot farther back, we gave the offense more of an alley to the basket. By moving the other foot up, we spread out, we look bigger, we bother them more.

(Diagram 6) Above this line we are going to **push you to the sideline.** We do that so we get an overplay and help. We contest every pass that goes in, whether to a post or a forward.

(Diagram 7) If you want to pass here, we will let you do that. We will allow you to **reverse the ball on the perimeter.** The feeling is that we can get there quickly enough to cover. On our forward overplay, we get all the way on top of the player with the front leg. Our back foot splits the middle of the body. We have the near arm extended and work at batting the pass away with that hand. The back hand is used as the **"bar arm" or the "feel arm."** We don't have the hand open because if we do, we grab. If the offense ever hits that arm, pivot, open up and slide two steps. If they can cover two steps, no one is going to beat them backdoor because of the pressure on the ball and the help on the backside. If you take away the guard-to-forward pass, you are really hurting their offense. Realistically, we feel we can take away the guard-to-forward pass on one side. If you reverse the ball guard-to-guard, we probably will not be able to get out to take away the one on the other side. We have made you use some time and change sides of the floor. If someone would do this every time, we would cheat out and cover.

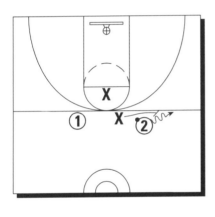

Diagram 6

Diagram 7

(Diagram 8) **Ballside, forward overplay.** The **weakside man** is in the lane only if he is quick enough to recover and challenge. We want support, but we don't tell him he must be in the lane. If the ball is above the head of the circle, the man covering the post is on the highside. If the ball goes below the free-throw line, he is going behind or on top to get there. The thing that is important on post defense is you must make the post shoot the ball. Don't give the center a layup or a dunk. Get between the post and the basket. Make that player shoot. If you really want to be hard, move him off the block. No one makes a 10' shot from the baseline with no backboard. That's about a 30% shot in the pros. Our main rule is **"do not run by the ball."** We put our arm bar on the fat roll. We want to be on top and the only contact we want to make is with the **arm bar.** If you lay on that center, and if he is strong, he is always going to beat you.

(Diagram 9) When the ball is passed like this, you must **decide how** you are going to get to the baseline side. Our rule used to be, and it really looked good, you would step through and over. It looked good until we played that big post player from Eastern Illinois. We couldn't do it. We couldn't go behind him because he would back us under the goal. We felt we had to go over the top. So, as the ball was in the air we would put our head in his belly and we'd spin. We never got a foul called. Know why? There is no signal for that. They won't call it. You will have to make individual rules for your players covering the post.

If he is quick, maybe he can go over the top. If he is slow, make him go behind. But, I would encourage you to stay between the man and the basket. That's the most important thing. If you don't have a dominant defensive center, it is imperative that you put pressure on the ball. Look again at the teams you play. Most teams only have one or two who can feed the post. You must figure a way to eliminate that.

Diagram 8

Diagram 9

(Diagram 10) If you are running the **forward overplay,** and he catches it, you must get your kids to **downshift and cover baseline.** If you have a dominant center who can block shots, then you can let that man go baseline. But, if you are playing straight man defense, you must keep people off the baseline. The defensive guard must drop off and toward the ball and go as deep as the ball.

(Diagram 11) Say that we get beat and here comes the **help man**. They drop it off and the defensive guard will get in there just in time to foul.

(Diagram 12) This kept happening so we changed our help principle. We don't help with the center, **we help with the ballside guard.** We drop the guard straight down to the baseline. No one makes the play where they pass from the baseline out to the ballside guard. They don't do it.

Diagram 10

Diagram 11

Diagram 12

(Diagram 13) **The 3-point goal** is driving me insane. It's almost like a touchdown. Against us, the guard would penetrate and they knew our rule for help, so they would pass to the wing fading. We can't change our rule on help, so we work hard at helping better. At practice we break down how we are going to help and recover.

(Diagram 14) **We never run by the ball.** And we never help uphill. If our guard is getting beat, the forward opens up and drops to help contain and is still able to recover. We feel that we can go two steps and still contest the 3. Next year, we are going to have one station where we will work on controlling the dribbler. Another station will be help and recover. A third thing will be our post drop. You can't do it halfway. You can't go halfway to the post to help. If you are going to drop off the wing, you must go all the way back as deep as the ball.

Diagram 13

Diagram 14

When I first started coaching, I had every drill that had ever been. There's nothing wrong with having drills as long as they fit what you are doing. I had kids who could do things in the structured situation of a drill, but when they had to recognize them going up and down the floor, they couldn't. We still do breakdown drills, but we run a lot of full-court situations and we coach on the move. Coaching in a scrimmage situation can be just as beneficial as all the breakdown drills. If I had to run drills, I would run the ones that Vegas runs. I went out and watched them in pre-season last year. Go watch some college teams in pre-season. They have a drill they do without the ball called **"slide, slide run." They go one-on-one full-court.** They slide two steps, work on their drop-step. When someone yells run, that means you're beat and you must turn and run. You must catch him, and get in position again. We then do it with a towel and a ball. We zigzag in backcourt. When you get to center court, you push him to the side and keep him there. We run the shell drill. You can work on everything there. Then run 5 on 4. It makes your kids communicate. You must point the ball and overplay the first pass ballside, and leave the farthest man from the ball alone. We have a hard time getting our kids to talk. This is a great drill to get your kids to communicate. Now, a rebounding drill. After you get back and establish pressure, defensive rebounding is the most important thing in the world. I've tried everything. Let your defensive rules take care of position. Then just go after the ball. Get your head under the ball and grab it with two hands. The only time we change that is if we find a team that has one great offensive rebounder, we may screen him on the spot.

(Diagram 15) You only have one man who is at a **rebounding disadvantage. He must go out and make contact.**

Diagram 15

(Diagram 16) Here is a **rebounding drill** that we start on the first day with two managers, a coach, and a line of players. The manager shoots it; he'll miss. The defense must get three in a row. He must rebound and outlet the ball to one of the managers. It's not easy. The first day you do this, you will only get six or seven shots completed. You will find that your team will get a little unity in this drill as they will begin to encourage each other. If the offensive man gets the rebound, he gets to keep shooting. If he hits, he gets to get back in the front of the line. We do call fouls on this drill. When a little man defends a big man, he quickly learns to screen on the spot. If the defense is big, he will go toward the ball. You get great effort out of this drill. We will also do 1/1, 2/2, and 3/3 and when we do 3/3 we will designate one of the wings to be in bad rebounding position.

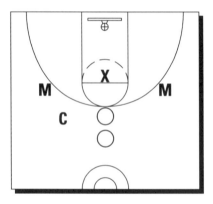

Diagram 16

I just sat in on a meeting in Kansas City where they wanted some input from schools our size. The main thing I learned is this. The best thing about sports is still working with kids and still spending time with coaches. Coaching is goofy now. They can say all they want, but it boils down to winning and losing. I envy you younger people. The one thing you lose as you move higher is you don't spend as much time with other coaches. Everybody is concerned about saving their job. Don't get so wrapped up in winning and losing that you miss making some great friends.

Chapter Eleven

MISSOURI BASKETBALL

Norm Stewart

All of us have a tendency, at times, to forget what our position is. I know I do. You, especially those of you who coach in high school, don't realize the significance of your job. The most significant person in my life, other than my parents and my present family, is my high school coach. I know many of you fill the same void for young people going to school right now. Don't forget what you are doing, and I just want to encourage you to keep that in mind. You are very important to young people.

I'd like to give you some background and then we will get into some defense. There are two theories in basketball. One is the **Execution of Fundamentals** and the other is **Tricks and Surprises.** We are very basic; you must understand that before we start. This is a very simple game. I think when someone is successful over a long period of time it has to do with two factors: **consistency and perseverance.** Something we do too much of is practice. Some guys are playing 100 games a year. We should be doing two things: teaching **rules** and working on **footwork.** Communication skills are based on your ability to say what you want to as succinctly as you can.

There are four things, when working with a basketball team, that you really need to understand.

1. When someone comes out to practice, it must be exciting. You must **challenge** him; show him some things. You must make it interesting so that he wants to come back. You must really put something into your practice. Immediately, that will tell you not to stay there too long. None of us likes to practice for three hours. Stay with him and shoot afterwards. You must make it an adventure. If you can't give it

to them today, they will find the adventure somewhere else. If they can find it in basketball, that will be plenty.

2. This is the most important until I get to the next point and then that is the most important. **Acceptance** is the word. You must get the players to accept you, and you must accept the players: for what he is as an individual, for what he is as a basketball player. I'm going to make mistakes. I'll tell you how the ratio will go. I will make one, you will make 10. (I'm older and have more experience.) I'll put up with your 10, you put up with my one. Now you have to get these players to **accept one another.**

    Even if they are all from the same community, they have different backgrounds, different values, different this and that. Once you get that, you have a chance to build a ball club.

3. In some way, every person on the team must feel successful. We call that **achievement.** If you have a drill, make it so that they will be successful. It doesn't have to be easy. Maybe the first day they can't do it. But, they will come back to it later. They must have **success.** It used to be the toughest thing in the world for me to tell a player that he couldn't play. But it is the best thing that you can do for him. If he can't play he will become **frustrated.** You must get him into a position where he can be successful. Some way you must be successful within the parameters of what your ball club can do. What is that success? You must know what that is.

4. You must be able to give recognition to everyone on your squad, and I don't mean false recognition. Let them know when they have done something good. Be specific. **Do not** go up to someone after a game and say: **"Nice game."** What does that mean? What is a nice game? **Be specific,** mention the **rebound total** or the **free throws made.** That means something. You are specific and giving recognition for being successful.

I want to talk about **defense.** You sit there and say, "You should have stopped a guy in 4.8 seconds," and I really appreciate you bringing that up. If you are going to play defense, no matter what type, you have to do these things. I will use simple words:

- **Basket.** Start at the basket and then **work out.** You must have good defense around the basket. **Post Defense.** You must have it, and you must play it with what you have. There is no unguarded layup.

- **Ball.** No one ever scored without it. You are going to guard the basket, and you are going to **guard the ball.** This is simple. How many times have you sat down with your team and gone through this? **Basket and ball.** Very simple.

- **Interrupt.** Don't let your man catch the ball where he wants to, when he wants to. Don't let him throw it where he wants to, when he wants to. **Interrupt the ball.**

- **Mistake.** Can you get your opponent to make a mistake? Are you more patient? You must have patience on defense, not just offense. Don't reach, don't grab, don't hold. A lot of times you don't have to win. All you have to do is let the other guy lose. You must be working while you are being patient.

- **Bad shot.** Can you get the other team to take a bad shot? **What is a bad shot?** If the best shooter on the team doesn't shoot it, it could be a bad shot. If they are running down the floor and they take an 18 footer, that could be a bad shot. I'd rather have that than a pass that goes out-of-bounds because there is conversion on the bad shot. We are going to lay it up. If they throw it out-of-bounds, their defense will get set before you inbound. You can force a bad shot. If you make a player shoot quickly, make a player shoot it over you, lack of patience, bad shot.

- **Second shots.** There are **no second shots.** You can't give up second shots, that's the start of offense.

You now have six principles of defense. Whether you are going to zone or you are going to press, you are going to do them over and over. You are always trying to accomplish these six things.

Individual Defense: You must work on these five things each day.

- **Stance.** Knee-hip; away from the ball, bent.

- **Position.** Guide the person. Away from the ball; intercept.

- **Footwork.** Lead foot; away from the ball, pointed to where the offense has to go. I must understand that when my player is away from the ball, he is going to want to go to the ball and that there may be a screen involved. But if there is just a naked play, I must understand that he must flash to the ball to catch it so I am able to stop it. I point my foot to the spot where he must come.

- **Hands and Arms.** Balance. Hands and arms have to do with the head. They are the two biggest factors of great athletes. Watch Michael Jordan. His head never comes forward. He has perfect balance. If you reach, your head must come out. His head stays in and he has balance. **Balance and quickness.** These are the two things all great athletes have. Away from the ball, use your **hands and arms.** Discourage your man from receiving a pass. Get your hands up. I think that hands are more important away from the ball than on the ball.

- **Vision.** On the ball. If I am playing defense on you, I am going to see you in total. You start waving at the ball; that's insignificant. When you get beat on defense away from the ball, one of two things will occur. You will either stand up, or you will lose your vision. The rest of it is insignificant. What happens when you stand up? Your man gets a step on you, and he closes the gap. He takes a step the same time as you get back down.

The other thing is **vision.** I want you to see your **man** and know where the **ball** is. I have some **"rankle points."** Did you ever see a player pass the ball to his teammate and his teammate didn't see it coming so he had to yell at him to warn him? Let me ask you a question. Why would it surprise a player if he had thrown the object that you play the game with? It seems to me that you would be surprised if your team position mate threw you his shoe, but not the ball. So, see the man and know where the ball is. Adjust your position until you can do that.

(Diagram 1) **Post Defense.** If the ball is in the middle of the floor, front the post.

(Diagram 2) If the ball is on either side in what we call the **corner** position, you **front** him. How do you front? When you front, body strong, hands up, and feet between his legs so that when the ball is thrown, you can go in the direction of the ball. (Put one leg between the legs of the post.) The rule is that when the ball is in the air or on the floor, it belongs to whomever wants it. Go get it.

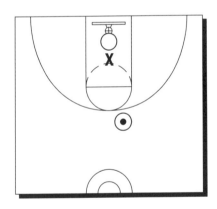 

Diagram 1   **Diagram 2**

(Diagram 3) The rest of the time we want to be on the **baseline side** with the right foot closer to baseline. Do not teach people to foul. I can't straddle the leg, but I can have a foot on either side of his foot. I don't want to be three-quarter on him, and I don't want to be one-quarter on him. I want to be half. I want him to have to move up the lane to receive the ball. I must recognize whether I can get the pass or whether I will wind up in position behind him.

When he catches the ball, as long as he has his back to me, I want a gap. When he turns and faces, I want to close that gap, keep my feet outside of his, keep hands up and get ready to move. I am going to need help. All I am going to do is hold the fort until I can get help. If he shoots, obviously, I'm blocking out.

When you are playing a wing, depending upon who you are playing and where you are playing, you must **decide** if you are going to take him baseline or take him back to the middle. You want to be **flexible**. There are some players who can really use the baseline. If you have a big man, you probably should go baseline because you can get your weakside help and fill your lane in a hurry. When the ball is at the point, we want to make that person declare to one side or the other. If you are playing a club that is all right-handed, it would be wise to take him to the left. We want to immediately establish which is the weakside.

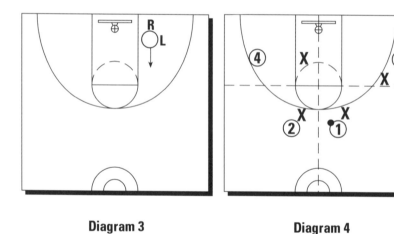

Diagram 3   Diagram 4

(Diagram 4) The ball is above the free-throw line. We split the court down the middle. We are talking about a basic 21' defense. We guide the dribbler (1) to the **outside**. The ball is above the line. I will draw an imaginary line between the ball and the next man, and I will have a defensive man so that he can get a hand in that line. If I want more pressure, I will put a foot in that line. I will do that with both 2 and 3, who are one pass away. The person guarding 4, who is two passes away, has contact with the lane. I can lob it to 4, but cannot pass it directly.

(Diagram 5) The ball is **below** the free-throw line at 3. The men guarding 2 and 4 are both in the center of the court. You have three things that you need in defense. You have the basket covered, the lane filled, and pressure on the ball.

To teach this we use the **four-man shell drill**. We put 35 seconds on the clock. We start to pass the ball and we make them adjust. Here are the rules. You can't catch it at the basket. You can't catch it in the middle of the floor. You must catch it outside the umbrella, which is what we call the three-point line. In order to teach this drill, you must teach two important ingredients of offense, spacing and timing.

(Diagram 6) They can start **low and pop out**, but you cannot allow them to catch the ball until they get as high as the three-point line. All the offense is doing is passing the ball. It teaches the offense movement, spacing, and timing.

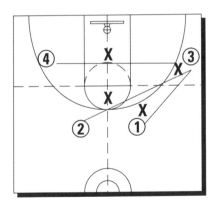

Diagram 5

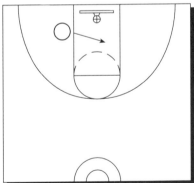

Diagram 6

(Diagram 7) When the ball is on the wing, the offense is trying to break to the baseline. The defense can't let the offense catch the ball at the **block** or in the **center** of the floor for 35 seconds. That is a simple reaction drill. You are working on the stance, the footwork, and the position of the hands and arms. Never let the weakside man **close the gap** coming to the ball. If he does, he will beat me. Stay one arm's length away. Beat him to the spot. Who has the advantage? The offense has the advantage. There are no shutouts.

(Diagram 8) We want to **widen** the people out. When 1 passes to 3, X1 must jump to the ball. He cannot allow 1 to make an inside cut. 1 must be made to go behind him. The helpside men are in the middle of the lane.

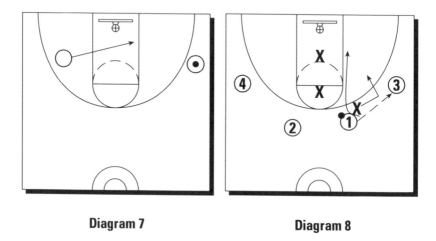

Diagram 7   **Diagram 8**

(Diagram 9) **Support and recover.** You can do this from any position. 1 drives. The defensive man guarding 3 must drop back and stop the drive and then recover. However, the defense must hold the position until the status of the man and ball has changed. In this aspect of the shell drill, the dribbler keeps trying to split the defensive people. The defense will support and recover.

(Diagram 10) **Vertical Screen.** 4 cuts to the basket, and 2 screens down for 4. 4 comes off the screen for the shot.

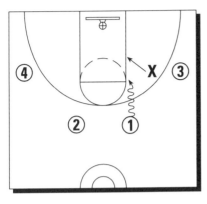

Diagram 9

Diagram 10

(Diagram 11) He may **curl or float** depending on whether the defense comes over the top or not. You can either go manside or ballside. The deeper in the lane the screen is set, the more apt the defender is to go manside. You go manside and you chase him out of there. So, he will curl. But you have help on the top from the man who is guarding the screener. That's when they talk. They must communicate.

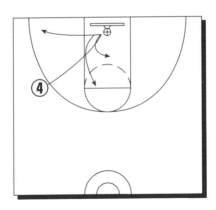

Diagram 11

(Diagram 12) The **toughest screen** in the game is on the lane. We start with the dribble; it gives the defense a chance to get set. 4 screens for 5. 5 must either go behind or over the top. It should come as no surprise that you are being screened. When 4 comes, don't stand there. Play the screen. Don't hit the screen. Miss the screen. Step in 4. Get on top of it. If X5 goes high, 5 will automatically go low. X5 will spin on 4. What are the two strongest parts of your body? Your hips and your shoulders. That's where your body strength is. Use your feet to put those into position. Don't hold with your hands. Put your hips on him and roll so both of them are covered.

Diagram 12

Chapter Twelve

FIELD GOAL PERCENTAGE DEFENSE

Roy Williams

We had to make a decision on how we were going to win games this year and our field goal percentage defense was 38.6 percent. The best way for us to win this year was for us to **stop you from scoring** and for us to **minimize your second shot opportunities.** Because of the dribbling rule, we couldn't get out and pressure the wings and get the steals. The best defensive principle is **"hand up on shot."** Take your best player, put him at the three-point line and have him shoot 100 shots. Then have him shoot 100 with you in front of him, just putting a hand up. They won't shoot as well. How many times have you seen kids reach in at their gut? That doesn't bother players at our level at all. We work on this several ways.

(Diagram 1) **"Closeout and Challenge."** The defense sprints out and breaks down the last step and a half and gets in the defensive stance, but he must challenge the shot. The shooter can shoot off the pass or take one hard dribble either way and shoot. If the defense can, we want the defensive man to go up with him. If not, stay on the ground, but get your hands up.

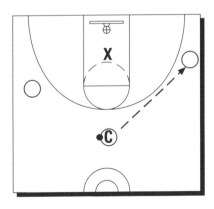

Diagram 1

(Diagram 2) **"Support and Challenge."** The coach drives. The defensive player must stop the dribble. The coach passes out to shooter and the defense must **closeout** as before.

(Diagram 3) **Inside,** the defense is in the middle. The offensive man is on the opposite block. The dribbler attacks and tries for the layup. X5 works on blocking shots. X5 faces out. The left arm is up, and the right arm is out forward.

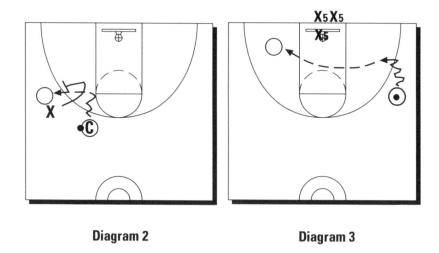

Diagram 2   **Diagram 3**

(Diagram 4) **"Pivot Defense."** If you get on the block, or below, we completely **front** you. We face the ball. We have one hand at our side, the other hand up. We want to lean back into you. So, if you leave, we know it. If you are one stride off the block, we will play you with the hand around in front. If the ball is **above** the free-throw line extended, that is a great position. If the ball is below the free-throw line extended, that's still a good position. But, when the ball gets below the line that the pivot player is on, then that's a tough spot.

(Diagram 5) Suppose we have one hand in front, and they try to throw the bounce pass to your inside hand, what do I do? We say, **"Don't go fishing for it and miss it."** We don't go over the top. We go behind you and **"wall it."** Now at least you must shoot over us. Get both hands up, and get the hands back. Exaggerate hands back. If you are able to go over the top and get around on the other side, you are going to beat that team anyway. But the good teams will ride you out and make the lob pass. By doing it that way, we push you lower to the baseline. Now, when you turn, the backboard isn't there.

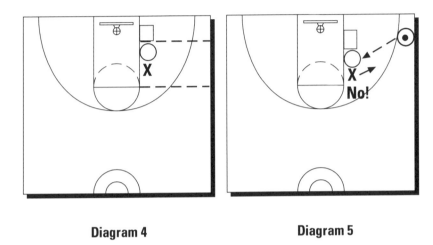

Diagram 4	**Diagram 5**

(Diagram 6) This is the middle and this is the sideline. We think there is a great difference in where you have the ball. If you have the ball in the middle, we are a little more **conservative** with you. If you have it on the sideline, we are going to do everything we possibly can to **keep** it over there, and we are going to try to run you where we have help.

(Diagram 7) We want the feet perpendicular to the sideline. We want to cut off a yard in either direction. We don't let you drive that yard. We do not let you drive to the middle of the court. We are going to stop any pass to the **top of the key,** and we are going to **deny** anything to the low post. We are going to keep you **on the sideline** when you get over there. When you are offense, would you rather have the ball in the middle of the court or on the sideline?

(Diagram 8) When we say **head-up,** we mean this. We don't want you between the man and the basket. We are running the ball into an area where we have help.

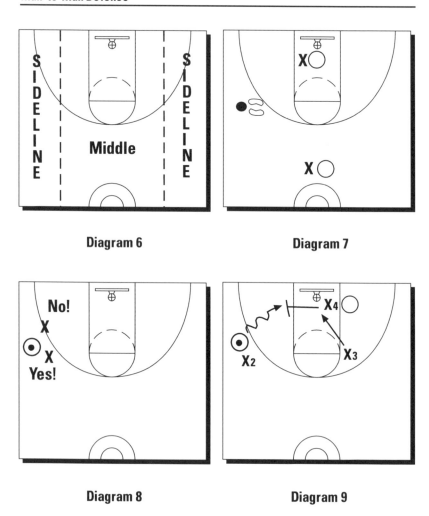

Diagram 6

Diagram 7

Diagram 8

Diagram 9

Diagram 9) If the defensive help comes from the weakside, we want him to come soon enough to stop him **outside the lane**.

(Diagram 10) If the help is on the strongside, and X4 is fronting, wait until the last instant to help. We don't want X4 to leave because X3 can't get there. If you can do these things, you will keep the field goal percentage down. We tell our players we want as much pressure as you possibly can apply, but we can't afford to get beat down the gut. If you can't handle it, you must drop off another half step. Each player must understand his limitations.

Our **first objective** on defense is to **steal the ball.** Our **second objective** is to let you take an **outside shot** over our hands and for us to get the **rebound.** Our **third objective** is to not let you do what you do every day in practice. If we come up against a very set team, they are going to have a tough time with this. We try to stay with **our philosophy.** We spend about 10 minutes showing what a team did against us last time. We are going to teach our defensive principles and that should take care of it. If not, we will find another principle and work on that. If we get ready to play somebody that runs a certain thing, we will emphasize that defensive principle.

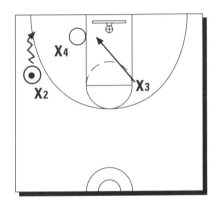

Diagram 10   Diagram 11

Question: How do you guard a player who can't shoot? Answer: We don't.

(Diagram 11) When we had Michael Jordan at UNC we played him there. He had to know where his man was, and he couldn't get a layup. But, you are talking about the greatest athlete I've ever seen. Jordan could guard the other four people. We gave him the other team's worst player. If you have one person who understands your defense better than anyone else, play him as a **rover.** Jam up the inside.

If we aren't playing a **rover,** we are getting after everybody. We don't want them to run their offense. I don't want them to do what they practice every day. If **we are better** than you are, we are going to scramble, trap, pick you up full-court, and try to make as many possessions as we can. If **you are better** than we are, we are going to try to make as few possessions as we can. If we are **about the same,** we are going to play our regular game and hope that it's our night. With teams that are about the same, we will give them personnel. We will list the penetrators and the shooters. We will differentiate between people. I think you can do that. We did that at the high school level. You must make some decisions. Is that man going to hurt you more putting the ball on the floor or shooting from the outside? We still try to **create tempo.** Our game doesn't change, but you must emphasize different things.

Question: If you are denial on the wing and there is penetration, what drill do you use to teach that?

Answer: (Diagram 12) Support at the point where you can still see your man and the ball. X2 must stop the dribbler and then get move on the pass. You expect the drive, but **closeout** so that if he goes up with the shot, you can get a hand up.

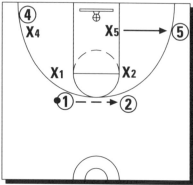

Diagram 12   **Diagram 13**

(Diagram 13) This is my favorite defensive drill. We let them make the first guard-to-guard pass. And we let them make nothing after that. When 1 has the ball, X4 is in denial, and X5 is off his man. When 1 passes to 2, X5 must sprint out to the denial spot and X4 moves to the help spot.

Question: When the ball is on the wing, do you **deny** the pass back to the point?

Answer: Yes. We try to do two things.

(Diagram 14) We have the **imaginary line** of ball. We want to be close to, or below, the line of the ball. We don't deny, unless it is **"dribble used."**

(Diagram 15) Now, if the man is **close,** then we will **deny** because I do not want the ball to change sides of the floor.

 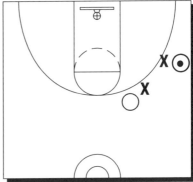

Diagram 14   **Diagram 15**

COACHES CLINICS

If You enjoyed this Practice Planning book, you won't want to miss these other great titles from the USA Coaches basketball library:

Practice Planning

Zone Defense

Girls' & Womens' Basketball

Match-Up Defense

Zone Offense

Developing the Fast Break

Special Situations

Pressure Defense: Volumes 1 & 2

Additonal information on other products in the USA Coaches library, including books, videos, and CD-ROMs, can be obtained by either calling 1-800-COACH-13 or faxing 1-314-991-1929.